How To Find Your
WAY BACK HOME

by

BESS S. PERMUT

PESHA PUBLISHING

P.O. Box 47484

Phoenix, AZ 85068-7484

Printed in the United States of America

Library of Congress Number 87-92255

DEDICATION

I dedicate this book to those souls who have walked this pathway before me, leaving signals and signposts for me to follow. May each of us who reads the contents of this book find ways to leave for future generations signposts that will be even more evident for the future generations to follow.

TABLE OF CONTENTS

CHAPTER   **Page**

PREFACE

In the summer of 1979 I was instructed to write this book, for which I had been gathering material for some thirty years. I became aware of the gifts God sought to bestow upon me as far back as 1947, and since that memorable year my mind was tuned to receive messages from higher levels of consciousness. My teachers and guides, as I affectionately term these higher minds, have been directing my awareness and have helped me bring comfort and solace to hundreds of people seeking answers to life's puzzles.

This book--a compilation of these teachings--lists and explains certain Universal LAWS that are of utmost importance. Living by these laws brings us closer to perfection in this plane.

After so many years of awareness, I find that NOW is the time to publish these teachings; this is the moment for which I waited, for it is NOW that the world needs a new direction, a new path to follow. Strife, unhappiness, and misery abound; the future looks uncertain. The lessons herein contained may open up new pathways, new avenues leading *Home. Home is with the Creator.*

Direct Contact through meditative thoughtwaves ensures that the words following are not of the writer, but are dictated directly to me by divine source. I have accepted these ideas as exact and truthful in order to help eradicate fear and despair.

You will find herein lessons to direct your thinking each day, to help overcome the fear of life, and to find fulfillment. Pathways are clearly marked upon the *Signposts.* Accepting these ideas will permit you to choose a happier life. We each one choose the life we lead. Every life is directed by inner thoughts, but we have choice. God always permits us to freely choose.

Doing HIS will is the best way of traversing the roads of life, free of pain and misery. Each one is sent to earth, or reborn ideally, for one thing: to simply dispel the *Karma* incurred during other lifetimes. Cast away the snares and mistakes of the past. How easily this is accomplished, simply by accepting *The Lord* as your partner.

The *Ten Commandments*, and the *Universal Law*, <u>*Love Ye One Another*</u>, have been decreed for all of mankind. Live by these laws and avoid stress. To live with disharmony and unforgiving heart is to live in vain. At some future time it will have to be re-lived again, and yet again, until the lessons are learned.

As a compilation of God's works and teachings, this book will surely appeal to those who are truly interested in learning new laws, experiencing new ideas, seeking new ways to cope with problems.

Herein may be found beauty beyond expression,

beauty in simplicity, just as from God's heart comes love and light. *Pure Love* will fill you with fresh insight and desires. You will experience the flash of a brilliant white light illuminating your soul. These are the feelings that come to me as I reread these lessons. Parables, *universal laws*, excerpts from the Bible, are all contained within, together with chapters pertaining to various facets of life, both in this world and beyond.

This book is written at the insistence of my teachers that the word of God be glorified and understood, that His people love and rejoice.

For life is good. Life is worthwhile. It is up to us to make it so.

FOREWORD

PART ONE

This book is written to bring to every human being a simple guide to everyday living, not to present a new religion. The world is allergic to the very word "religion." This book presents a new way of living--a new set of rules to live by. You will be living the golden rule of God as God meant life to be lived.

In selling cosmetics, one never sells the product because a woman is ugly and needs something; one sells the product because it will help her maintain her beauty. We seek the people who are blind, stumbling, ready to plunge over the cliff--they are perceived as ugly: but in this work we perceive them as whole and needing just a bit of change. We recognize no chastisement: we see everyone as God meant them to be, and thus we can help them make it true. There are no inferior beings. All are whole; all are good. A child who is naughty, if told repeatedly he is good, will soon be a good child. Seek out the good qualities of the person, never the bad. He will soon see himself, see his own discords in comparison with his good harmony. Never say, "I recognize a miss in your motor," so to speak; better to observe, "I notice you keep your car in good condition." It really pays! Your friend might say, "Didn't you notice? The motor is missing a little; I have to get it fixed." Just make him proud to own such a car and thus he will seek perfection. He will take better care of it in the future. Nothing was ever learned by pointing out someone's flaws to them. The wisest of us can never accept criticism. This must be one of the pillars of your foundation. If criticism is needed, start first with two compliments. Close your ears to discord. Try to live love. Build up; never feel free to remove one brick from another's foundation. Diplomacy is to be used with love.

If you see through the eyes of love, sinners appear to be saints. They themselves will admit to being wrong. Counter with, "So what? You are reborn each day. The past is gone; the future is a far distant time. This is the day to live as you want to live. Your yesterdays will be washed clean. Your tomorrows will loom ahead as bright as pinnacles shining in the sunlight. Every day is your jewel to dull or polish to the brightest hue. Every day becomes a song. The future is eagerly awaited. When anything distracts you, remind yourself, *This is My Day!* This little insignificant trouble will not mar my jewel."

Make a chart of your emotions. Notice how they are up one day, down another. Keep this record for a month. Then study your chart and observe that it travels in a cycle. So it does for everyone. When a bad day comes, shrug it off with this thought: "*This is one of my bad days. I can expect a gloomy outlook, but I know it is not the world turning against me. It is just my cycle. I will take no heed and will not let this disturb me; I will just think a positive thought."*

At first you may have many gloomy days. Try to change them; by anticipating them you can prepare yourself to act more positively in order to control them. Start the morning with this prayer: *"God bless my efforts this day. Let me make the best and most of every opportunity that comes to me. Give me, Father, all the things I need for this day."* At night before retiring: *"Thank you, Father, for all the blessings of this day. Protect me and keep me through this night."* When in trouble or doubt: *"I am God's child; nothing can harm me! Father, strengthen my convictions."*

Teach these simple prayers to your children, that they, too, may walk in God's way. When you see beauty, thank God for the ability to see it. When you see ugliness and despair, ask God to send blessings. Go through the garden of life strewing roses of beautiful thoughts and deeds. Thank God for everything that passes your way. Such peace, such happiness as you have never known will be yours. You will find you are the vessel of God's love--a living chalice of His goodness and generosity. Guard your tongue and your mind--don't waste them on discord or unworthy thoughts or deeds. Live today as though there will be no tomorrow. Say the good things, do the good deeds that come into your heart today, as though it were the last day of your life on this earth. Sincerely try each day to make someone happy--just one person--and happiness will flow from you and back to you in a stream of God's love and good will. It is not enough to pray or think good thoughts. We must create good thoughts and put them to work for us. We must learn to live love. We must feel love of all things; love of our opportunities, love of everything that comes our way. Life will then take on added flavor, if we love life itself.

We don't mean to imply you will be "holier than thou." No, you will have such a broad understanding of human nature that all who encounter you will wonder at the peace you bring to all who are around you.

When you meet someone who is living negatively, who irritates you no end, ask God to show you how to help this person. Before criticizing, say to yourself, "Let me judge this man by God's standards, not my own." If we could follow this maxim, we would find no one wanting. To God we are all perfect. This is God's way; this is the way He meant us to be before religion was interpreted by man of small soul. We can have no true conception of God's laws through interpretation that has been made small and mean. That is not the Father's way at all. God does not teach fear, hatred, or retribution. He teaches us to live outside ourselves. He teaches, "You are your brother's keeper. Fill your hearts with great love for everything."

The disciples did not go about in sackcloth and ashes. They strode proudly without fear. They ate well, slept well, and preached to mankind to "live and let live." Much of God's teachings of pure gold have been changed to gloss, so it is no wonder we live with black hoods over our heads and cannot see the light.

Just imagine the greatest love you have ever known. That is but a poor imitation of the love God holds for us. There is no crime so awful that He cannot forgive. He is the true scale of justice. He knows what lies in every heart. He alone can pass judgment. Weigh this well: *"Never judge lest ye be judged."* This guide to living will teach you to live proudly.

Be not afraid to love. Love freely. Let love flow like a river from you. The more you love, the more you are capable of loving. In this manner you can do no wrong-- your life will be a symphony of delight.

Forward- xxx

PART TWO

Are you happy with your life? It is as simple as flipping a coin to change. Everyday people who understand *Universal Laws* succeed easily. *Universal Laws* are basic laws--truth--truisms that have existed since time began.

In truth nothing is new; there is just a continuation of thought, deeds, and actions from the Source from the beginning through to eternity. The words may be changed and masqueraded so they appear new and different, but essentially they remain the same old *Universal Laws*, the same truths handed down generation to generation since the beginning of time and understanding. The Supreme Being or Power that guides and directs us leads us to believe and consider reincarnation. Have you considered reincarnation as giving many answers to why we are living? Do you understand why you are in truth living at this period of time? Why are we here? Do you believe that your lifetime on earth is an aimless wandering where you simply put in your time, or are you certain there is purpose--a well-planned existence awaiting each of us who have many lessons to learn, many debts to repay. First, ask yourself why you are here. Search deeply within your consciousness for the answer. It will not come overnight, but do not despair or give up hope of knowing or learning what your destiny really is all about. Meditation will help to clarify your thoughts and help you to understand why you live and the purpose of living.

Having accepted the idea that life has purpose, you must then set forth to discover and execute that purpose to find the pathway leading you back home to the Supreme Being and everlasting life. In so doing, you are executing the deeds needed to repay the karmic acts from centuries ago and in other lifetimes. Now you are able to instill in your mind the wisdom required to fulfill the covenant made centuries ago that you presented before the council of the Supreme Beings. You may have wandered aimlessly, not knowing your destiny, living without fear of retribution. Your true destiny now can be accomplished. In truth, many never know what is required to fulfill their destiny. They do not know how to seek--how to look within, to learn the truth about themselves.

The Big Bang

There is ample evidence in revitalized life in the hereafter. There is destiny to perform; otherwise, why would reincarnation occur time after time? You must allow yourself time to observe the truth about the *Laws* that were established centuries ago. There is no mystery as to where men came from--one explosion upon the mountain of good hope brought us forth. Evidence or remains of this "Big Bang" is felt in civilization that still exist. It is only a matter of learning how to view the evidence of *truth everlasting.* Evidence of living everlasting lives still exists. One has only to learn to explore one's mind for answers. The Lord confirms *truth everlasting* when we learn the steps needed to assure a relationship with Him.

We must instill into your minds these thoughts: To live solitarily high on a mountainside is to be lost. We must mingle with all of mankind, not set ourselves up as special or different, for we belong to one of the whole. We are of the one substance that formed us all. From the origin of time, man singled himself out and sat upon the throne. Thus not understanding his predicament, man finds himself today without wit or humor--and mankind is lost. He must learn to laugh at himself, at his own mistakes, but he must learn to take his mistakes to heart also and learn the lessons therein. Therefore, it is one thing to be able to laugh at oneself, but it has little meaning if we do not learn the lesson of our mistake. Therein, laugh and be jolly. Don't appear dour today; come out of the wilderness and into the light--and enjoy life.

PART THREE

Personal Experiences

When I was a small child we lived in the country, where my father owned a general store. The store was attached to our home so that I was able to spend a lot of time with my father. As was my habit, I loved to nap under a certain lilac bush during the spring and summer when the earth was warm. I would nap or just daydream as I watched the clouds above forming all kinds of shapes. The sky fascinated me. My parents could not understand why I chose that particular mode of bed for napping instead of my own comfortable one. I referred to this lilac bush as "my lucky place," for I had beautiful dreams there. At other times I would visit with little angel children--my pretend friends. They were very real to me and I carried on long conversations with them.

One afternoon I awakened from my nap and ran to

tell my father about the strange cars I saw flying through the sky with people riding in them. I described them in great detail. Since the year was in the late twenties, little was known about planes in our area. I described to him the jets as we now know them, and how the jet stream looked. I told him that the planes almost looked like they were burning, and left a trail of smoke behind. I related to him that when they took off to go into the sky, they went straight up into the air.

My father was accustomed to my fantasies. He just patted my head and said, "You must have had an interesting dream, but we know cars can't fly like birds through the sky, don't we?"

Some time later I told my father about a dream I had in which I had seen our barn completely engulfed in flames; our car had been burnt and completely destroyed, and the barn was a complete loss. Exactly as in this vision, two weeks later the barn was consumed by flames and the car was indeed destroyed. It was only through the help of all the wonderful neighbors that our home had been saved from destruction. Also with their help, a new barn was built several days later.

My mother was accustomed to my coming to her and saying, "Mrs. Jones (or Mrs. Smith) is coming to visit this afternoon." At first my mother would toss such statements off as my imagination running rampant again. She would usually answer me by saying, "Mrs. Jones can't come to see us in the middle of the day. She has a small baby" . . . or . . . "this is the day to wash." But true to my prediction, the neighbor would show up at our door. After a while, when I told my mother about these impending visits, she would prepare for the visitors and no longer doubted my word.

My mother constantly warned me not to relate any of my dreams or visions to anyone else for fear they would laugh at me or think me demented. For many,

many years, because of this warning my predictions were suppressed. I used my gift only to safeguard my family and friends until the incident occurred at the Pearl Harbor Navy Yard in 1942. It was as though a floodgate was opened and all the information for this book came flowing through. Then I realized I could no longer withhold the knowledge, and my wisdom came forth. The lessons that follow were brought about in this same fashion. I feel this gift is a blessing--not for my use alone, but to be used for all of man-kind. Over the years I have seen much of this information given to classes and to individuals, and it has helped them find the road that leads them back to the Father. Many have said it has given them the reason for being--the reason for their lifetime on earth.

Personal Experience: Spring of '42—Pearl Harbor

In the spring of 1942, as a statistician at Pearl Harbor, an experience firmly convinced me that life had purpose and delineated my purpose for me. On this particular morning a friend offered to drive me to the Navy yard by car; usually I rode the bus. The ride brought me to my office much earlier than usual. As was my habit each morning, I dusted my desk and went to the window of my second floor office to shake out the dust cloth. I enjoyed looking up at the beautiful blue sky that was constantly filled with fluffy white clouds. On this particular morning as I looked up at the sky I saw Army and Navy planes practicing their simulated dog fights over the Navy yard. As I continued to watch, I was shocked and completely horror-struck as I watched two of the planes collide and come tumbling down in flames. Not only were the crews killed, but the planes landed upon a "Leaping Tuna"[1] filled with Navy workers arriving for the day. I could hear the screams and moans as clearly that moment as I have continued to hear them

---

[1] A "Leaping Tuna" is a vehicle used to transport workers around the Navy yard.

for these many years. I stood at the window screaming, not realizing I was screaming. At that moment I thought I heard softly spoken words saying, *"These are your brothers and sisters. Why are you standing there instead of going to their aid? Don't you know every man is his brother's keeper? From this day hence you must always be thus to all of mankind. Now you know that is your purpose in life."*

Where did the voice come from? Who was directing me to go and help the others? It was then I began to wonder and ponder over the events of that day, the offer of a ride without which I would not have been at that window at that time. I have since learned to accept through this and other experiences that we are guided and directed somehow to find and perform our destiny on this earth.

Personal Experience: Did God send an angel to help me?

During the depression of the thirties my family lived

in Columbus, Ohio. After finishing high school, I won a scholarship to Ohio State University. I was unable to attend the university as my mother had been left a young widow and there were no funds to pay for books, clothing, or carfare. Therefore, I started to look for work in order to continue my education. I was untrained for office work, and soon learned there were no jobs to be had.

Through my high school counselor I learned of a very kind lady who sometimes financed needy youngsters. She loaned me enough money to take a business course at Bliss College. It was considered a fine school and the graduates were easily placed.

When I finished my course I was shocked to learn that there were many well-trained people being interviewed for the positions I was seeking. Why should an employer hire a novice when he could easily hire someone with many years of experience? Feeling very dejected after one particular interview, I went back to the school, thinking I would simply practice typing to keep up my skill rather than go home in defeat. We were allowed to use the typewriters at school during lunch break any time.

The typing room was empty except for one young man, and soon I found myself pouring out my heart to him because I needed work so badly. He asked if I knew that the State of Ohio was taking applications for the newly formed Liquor Control Department. He gave me the address and all the instructions--when and where to go to apply. I thanked him for his kindness and patience and for being the first positive person I had spoken to. I introduced myself to him and asked his name and where he worked. He was a reporter for the Columbus Dispatch. He, too, had graduated from Bliss College and said that he also stopped by often at the noon hour to practice his typing.

I hurried to the address he had given me. When I was finally interviewed, I was asked for references, and I gave the name of the lady who had loaned me the money for the business course. I did not realize how prominent a person she was until I saw the expression on my interviewer's face. She assured me If my friend would vouch for my character, I would hear from them within two days.

As I boarded the streetcar for home I felt elated, bathed in a warmth as though I somehow was certain the position would be mine. True to the intuition, the next day the telephone rang, asking me to report for work.

I wanted to thank the kind young reporter immediately, so I called the Columbus Dispatch, only to be told they had no one by that name working for them. I began calling the other newspapers in town, thinking I had made a mistake. Each newspaper informed me that they had no one by that name working for them. I went back to Bliss College and inquired at the registrar's office for his phone number or address, but was told that the school had never had such a person registered as a student. I was in total shock. Who was this young man who helped me and directed my footsteps at a time of such distress? He certainly was responsible for my finding a job when jobs were hard to come by. I have concluded after many years that he was one of God's angels who came to help me at my time of need.

Throughout all of my life, when I have been in need God has sent me that which I needed.

How I Found My Way Back

I found myself living high on the mountaintop where the Lord lives. Should I gain wisdom or should I continue to live solitary in the valley below? The answer depended on me. I sat down and pondered the answer, and soon the truth became manifest before my eyes. I was sent to earth to teach others how to find the Father. True, the wisdom on earth is manifested through the mind and I found wisdom waiting within my own mind, waiting for centuries to be released in order to help others find the way safely back home to the Father.

The experience I am describing is the loss of my own father in this time of life. When I lost him, I thought it was the end of my life--my way of life--indeed, my life itself. Instead, I started searching for my father. I did not accept the fact that he was dead, and the thought that he was lost to me forever was incomprehensible. It did not make sense to me; such a vital man to be just put into the earth and vanish forever. I started looking for him. What baffled me most was that no one could answer my question about truth everlasting. Does mankind live on forever, or just in our memory? Do our minds live on? I decided to look elsewhere and soon I received hope, for I read of a mystic who could communicate with the dead. I looked to that source of wisdom and, lo and behold, I found the answer to my own seemingly unanswerable problem. I found the Father!

Yes, through searching for my father, I actually found the Father, for they were one and united into one. This was difficult for me to understand. As I stood before the Father in my meditation, I asked to see my real father, with whom I had lived on this earth plane. The answer came: "He is busy learning how to communicate with you through your mind's eye. Try to envision his standing here talking with you." Immediately I began to imagine my father beside me. Wonderful things soon began to happen. I felt secure again; I was comforted again and again. By wandering into the realm of probability seeking my father, I learned many answers. Later on, I again sought to speak with my father. This time I was told he was educated beyond my realm of thinking or probability, that his union with the Lord was complete and he wanted me to understand that his purpose, in my life, had been to teach me how to find the *Father*. He has come back into our lives to teach us thoughts like these--a renewal of spirit, a reawakening to our purpose in this lifetime.

My purpose in this lifetime is to teach others how simple it is to find the Father. What is your purpose?

*Forward-*1

CHAPTER 1

MEDITATION

Meditation is the Gateway leading us to the Kingdom of Heaven. Meditation is the secret of communicating with the Supreme Being or your higher self. There is no mystery to meditation; everyone can achieve it. Today, unfortunately, many people are making millions of dollars teaching people how to meditate without the pertinent explanation of "why" they should learn. You will learn that meditation raises you to your higher spiritual self and acts as a reward as each person learns to know himself and find himself. Meditation is the first step in learning to fulfill that which you came to do. You will learn the principles behind meditation, how truly simple it is, and what you can receive from it.

Meditation is also used to lower blood pressure by some medical men. This process is old--centuries old, as old as recorded history. That, indeed, is the purpose of this book: to give to each of you (since the Supreme Being sees and creates us all equal) the opportunity to teach yourself how to meditate. When we pray we are asking the Supreme Being to help us ease our troubles and problems. When we meditate we are listening for answers and directions. When you are truly in touch with a higher consciousness (regardless of what you might call it), then you realize you are never truly alone. This is one of the basic Universal Laws: We are one unto the Supreme Being. We are all brothers and sisters, regardless of race, creed, or color. We are all loved equally, and were meant to enjoy our lives and have that which we need. (This theme will be explained in detail in the chapter titled "Visualization.")

Step #1 in Meditation

Please allow yourself to feel at peace and in harmony with the world when you enter the room or place where you are going to meditate. If there is a phone, take it off the hook. Lock your doors so you will not be abruptly disturbed. Inform your family and friends what time each day you will be occupied with your meditation so you will not be disturbed. Then find a comfortable position. Some sit; some lie down. Others go into all types of yoga positions, but what is basically necessary is that you find a comfortable position. It is recommended if you sit in a comfortable chair that you take your shoes off, place your feet firmly upon the floor, and cup your hands--palms up--upon your lap in a comfortable position as though you expected something wonderful and beautiful to be placed into your hands. At this point I ask my students to repeat the Lord's Prayer and visually surround themselves with light while asking for God's protection as we enter into the beautiful garden. One can visualize oneself in any location that makes one happy--a place that has much meaning to you. For me, it is a garden. We always go into the beautiful garden and wait by the gate until we feel ready to enter; then slowly walk down a pathway to a lily pond that is located in the center of the garden. The lily pond has a water fountain in the center of the pool. It is when you approach this pool that you stop and gaze into the pool, watching the drops of water descend into the bottom of the pool. Try to keep your mind clear of all the problems and thoughts that have disturbed you, saying "one" each time your mind wanders so as to bring yourself back to watching the water. Soon you will feel or see a teacher come into your mind's eye or your picture, and it is then you must be quiet and listen with your mind's eye to what is being said. Many times this is not accomplished for quite a time. Do not allow yourself to become discouraged if someone does not appear immediately or if you do not hear a voice speaking within your mind's eye. It will happen if you will continue. Be at peace and be patient.

One seems to become revitalized during this period of meditation and my masters have often told me that it is during this period of time and while we sleep that all negativity is eradicated from our minds and beautiful positive thoughts are placed into the trough of our minds.

During these periods of meditation, which should last only twenty minutes at a time, we are shown pictures and colors. Many times past lifetimes are flashed upon the screen of your mind; we are allowed to see that which we have come back to correct in this lifetime. It is important to remember at this time that we have chosen our lives; so let us not wail or rail at it, but learn how to flip the coin to change and make our lives worthwhile.

It is no accident that your family belongs to you. Each of you chooses one another to repay past debts (karma) or to relive and help the other to find the pathway back. With meditation, very often you will be shown why you chose the life that you did and how you can make it work so that you can evolve to the higher state of consciousness all of us strive to find.

Select a certain time each day, as though you have a date for that time, and make a promise to yourself and your teachers that you will be there every day. Soon you will feel that your life is incomplete if you miss a session of meditation. You will begin to feel re-energized when you finish with your meditation, and solutions to problems will be brought to you as well. You will wonder why you never thought of these solutions before; they seem so simple. It is while you meditate that you allow your spirit to sing, soar, and be joyous, to escape imprisonment. You are rewarded with the answers to what you thought to be impossible. So accept the responsibility each day of allowing time for your date, and be rewarded with the greatest gift the Supreme Being can bring into your life: peace of mind, health, happiness, and a harmonious relationship with the universe.

A second method of meditation is used by many of the students simply by making believe that they are watching a TV screen. They get comfortable as described before and visualize themselves sitting down before a TV screen. Soon, within their minds, they see objects upon the screen; it then progresses into hearing and seeing with total recall when they finish their twenty minutes of revitalization. Whichever manner you choose to use, you must dedicate yourself to a daily date--an appointment, so to speak--and to receiving only the highest of thoughts so as to commune with your higher spiritual self and get the answers and truths needed to fulfill your destiny.

Meditation is the answer--meditation is the pathway. Which way you enter into the spiritual way of life depends on you. You can accept truth and enlightenment in your life, or destroy the opportunity given unto you to restore life everlasting within your lifetime. Which shall it be? It's up to you and you alone. Make that dedication, and know and fulfill your destiny.

Silence is Golden

Since the beginning, man has sought out other men with whom to communicate directly through thought transference. Today on the continent of Africa there remain from prehistoric times tribes who use a mental communication whereby they are able to send messages to other tribes thousands of miles away. Some religious orders--until this very day under vow of silence--are able to communicate and understand each other through pure thought.

Perhaps once in time, in the beginning, the Father sought us out and implanted pure thought into our minds. We each one understood exactly what he said to us, and we transferred these thoughts to others through a kind of brainwave or mental transference. We named it "telepathy."

Once, long ago, a kingdom of men reigned supreme because they used this sort of communication and could relay messages to far away places without overt physical means of communication. We have lost that art, together with much of our freedom of truth, because we have lost the art of mental telepathy. The excuse we use is that the sound waves were often inaccurate. A lame excuse, for such thought transference prevailed long centuries ago. Thus, the truth was made manifest. There was then no excuse for mis-translations. Much of the histories of people, the understanding of truth itself, is distorted today because of mispronunciation or translation of the original thought.

Education is a must. Man must arm himself with understanding that silence is golden. From many aspects we regard silence as an art of communication through trance meditation, and so forth, but it is silence that manifests truth heard during periods of silence. Today we accept the mortal concept of timely wisdom; that which is taught by man and interpreted by man. We do not accept the moral truths that were manifested centuries before the birth of Christ, or even before Moses.

Truth is little understood today because man buries his head in the sand and refuses to listen. He refuses to be quiet, silent, until apathy overtakes him. Apathy exists among ministers as well as their fellow congregates. A blindfold is used by them to disguise the real truth, and thus the messages direct from the Father are not known because of man's ignorance. Accept the magic wand extended to you today. Use your mind; set it free. Let it roam and wander where it will, so it may hear the truths as were spoken in the beginning. Cascade these thoughts into action. Live according to the Golden Rule in the Scriptures. We must learn how to handle truth. Ignorance makes enemies by excluding many of God's children. The pure sense of truth holds that all men are God's children. Shut out hatred and discrimination; select a second time in history to avoid hypocrisy. Don't act according to false teachings and training; act with heart and understand the truth--that God Almighty serves all mankind, whether he be white, Southern Baptist, Christian, Jew, Mohammedan, or Buddhist. God serves them all. He listens to them cry out for justice and truth equally.

Silence is golden. Retrieve the art of listening. Salute the Father each morning upon arising with these thoughts: *"Oh Heavenly Father, I salute you this morning for the glory of thoughts you produce within my mind. You send forth to me this day this message of truth, to salute you and all of mankind. I shall bless all mankind, and in so doing send him higher into the kingdom, for it is through these thoughts that the single purpose of life is manifested."*

Through love for his fellow man, mankind establishes a base of recognition and contact with the Almighty, the base of understanding man's purpose on earth. Salute the Lord each morning with these words: *"I have saluted the Lord this morning in your name also."* Silence is golden. If you are silent and listen to the Lord's light beaming into your mind, you can recall your destiny; for He stands there reminding you each morning what you are destined to accomplish. Truly know this: each man has one more step to take with this knowledge, and--further down the road--one more step to reach the top. If you can, imagine yourself reaching the top, achieving the top of the mountain, away from all mankind, seeking advice from the Father. He will instill into your mind reality worth listening to. With this expression of truth you can and will manifest the truth everlasting for all of mankind to follow on into eternity. Otherwise, you have lost the opportunity of your lifetime on earth.

Meditation- 14

CHAPTER 2

VISUALIZATION

In the beginning you were asked if you were happy with your life, and you were told that it was as simple as flipping a coin to change it. We will now go into details that you can easily follow to accomplish a happier life, providing all that you need--whether it be health, wealth, etc.

We must first have faith in the Father or the Supreme Being, and know through Him that all things are possible. We must, each morning upon arising, continually repeat the following to ourselves: *"The God in me can accomplish and overcome whatever I may face this day, for I am a part of all that is."* We have now set our course for the day; we have cleared the fear and apprehension we might have felt. The next important step is to know exactly what you want, for we set thoughts into action and motion and <u>thoughts</u> are <u>things</u>--mind over matter, so to speak. Take your time and determine exactly what you want, and then set the mental picture into action.

A mental picture is a form of photography. Since we want a positive life and want to bring to ourselves the beautiful life, we must not accept negative pictures. When an unwelcome thought occurs, producing a negative picture, we must wipe it out. If a word is spoken that makes you envision an unpleasant picture in your mind, you must be emphatic about it and affirm, *"This does not belong to me; this is alien to me. Cancel it. Cancel it."* Thus, you do not acknowledge or accept the negativity, and this will stop it.

The source of negative thoughts, of course, is a negative mind, which can create unpleasant and unsatisfactory events in your life. You must try by the above affirmations to have a positive mind, and when you slip back into your old negative patterns you must take yourself in hand and repeat the affirmations noted in the above paragraphs.

Be absolutely certain that you want what you visualize, and make sure that you see the picture of what you desire moving. The reason so many of our prayers or visualizations do not materialize is that we do not make them move; there is no action. See yourself making that last payment on your home, your car; see yourself standing before audiences talking to them, enjoying yourself as you do so--if that is part of what you desire. See the exact amount of money needed to run your home being placed into your hand each week. Whatever it is that you need, visualize it. Eat it, sleep it, and talk about what it is you want.

You must concentrate upon the thing you most desire and hold a positive picture of this desire. You must have the faith that the Superior Being can create anything and that He is a bountiful Father, that you are in truth one unto Him, that it can be accomplished. Remember, you must know exactly what you want, visualize it, and hold a positive picture, knowing it can and will come about. It is in this manner that you picture perfect health, happiness and prosperity for yourself and those you love.

A vivid imagination is of particular value to the student of truth. When you decide upon a thing and imagine it, you send the photo or image into the ether and it comes forth as a happening. First the thought, then the word, then the picture; then out of the substance comes the final realization of that which you have pictured.

If it is money you need--not so that you might save or collect, but truly need--you must picture yourself actually counting that money and at the same time giving praise and thanks for the money. If it be clothing or a car that you need, bless the old car, the old coat or dress, or whatever piece of clothing you need to replace, for the good the old one has done. In being grateful and thankful for all that you have been blessed with, you receive that which you need. In giving thanks for the blessings you hope to receive, acting as though you have already received the blessing completes the picture and, thus, you have set into motion the reality of your dreams being fulfilled.

This is a form of fantasy or make-believe which may sound foolish to some, but ask one who has been successful in his field of endeavor and he will tell you he set a goal and worked with all his heart and soul to accomplish it, which in reality is the only way to succeed. This is success based on the mental plane of expression. The mental picture is more lasting if it is accompanied with prayer.

First, sit in a comfortable chair or get into a

comfortable position, then use this statement: *"I give praise and thanks to Thee, O Father, that You are bringing forth this perfect picture to me. I know it pleases You to see Your children happy, healthy, with peace of mind. Teach me, O Father, to love, that I might create beauty, health, happiness and material worth for all of Your children, as well as myself"* The prayer you have just spoken is for the fruits of pure spirit. If you ask for these things sincerely, all things will be added. It is not a sin to pray for material needs when in need, but it is a broken law to pray for these things first, last, and always.

You turn to the Almighty Father first, and then the *Universal Law* starts to work. It works in a preciseness that man does not understand, but only if you are positive, knowing that your needs will be fulfilled. You are then able through your positive mind to tune into health, happiness, peace of mind, and prosperity. If you turn to the negative thought, you turn to sin, sickness, and other negative aspects not necessary to bear in this lifetime.

Remember each day to say after you start your visualization, *"I am one with the Father with whom I live, since He lives in my mortal temple; therefore I shall lack for nothing, ever."*

Making a Success of All Living

"May God grant me blessings on all my endeavors."

Take God as your partner in all you do. You were not meant to stumble along alone. The simple formula of surrendering all your being to God, then walking with Him, will create amazing effects. Bless every task you undertake. If it is something you dislike, bless it; give it to God! Ask Him to send you the power to flow with it. You will find yourself not only getting through the dreaded task, but feeling jubilant over mastering a negative condition. If you bless continually, your thoughts will be sent out into the ether to become a flow of power. Just try to realize how powerful a blessing is: it is one of the strongest ideas a human brain ever transmitted. Everyone at some time has experienced a wave of intense hate: its powerful vibration is one-hundredth that of a blessed thought. Bless every negation, be it a condition, a person, or a policy. In the morning, ask God's blessings on all you encounter that day, everything and every person that touches your life. In so doing, you release a flood of God's love. Can you see that by so doing you are doing your small part to make this world a better place to live? Multiply this by one hundred or one thousand, and see that God's roses of love and tolerance will soon be embracing the world. Now as never before, we need the gentleness of His loving hand working through us. We need to pull up the weeds of hate, intolerance, and prejudice, and plant flowers of love.

In God's vibration, all is whole. There is nothing but good. When you find bad conditions or unhealthy minds, it means lack of faith. Only this can explain the chaos in which we are now living. Let every man practice love, and we all live. Take God as your partner in everything. Ask His advice and seek His wisdom. Take Him as a partner in every enterprise, even in little things. Ask His help in everything; then pay your partner God His share by loving. You will never regret it!

"All that is given in God's name shall be blessed and multiplied."

Visualization- 24

CHAPTER 3

LOVE

"Love ye one another" is the golden rule. The words flow through our minds and our bodies. God's love flows through us as the rays of the sun flow through the universe. The sun shines freely upon us without choosing favorites. It shines freely upon everyone. How do we dare to question the worth of those who receive warmth and its light? As the sun shines, so God loves. God's love flows freely to all; to the just, to the unjust, to the deserving, to the undeserving, to saint and sinner alike.

God's love pours over us, awakening us to life, just as the sun brings forth the bulbs and leaves in the proper time and gives strength and color to the trees and the growing plants. Similarly, the animals and the vegetables and the minerals that lie below the surface of the earth all partake of God's love.

Can you not see how God planned the universe for us even before we came into being? It was He who planned the sun, the moon, the water, and the minerals found buried in the earth that we are now using millions of years later. That is God's love. Yes, God's love is the most important thing, the one thing we can be sure of. What kind of father would want to abuse, destroy, or end a child's life? He loves us; He is always close to us. Therefore, we too must turn to all of mankind and say, "I love you." You don't even have to say it aloud, but say it mentally. When you see someone helpless or suffering in a wheelchair, or, for example, someone who is blind, always reach out mentally with your love and bless them. In that way you are simply passing on God's love. You are one with Him, thus an extension of Him.

When we truly know ourselves and how we relate to God, then and only then can we extend that true love that we receive from the Father. It is when we recognize the oneness, the spiritual or conscious union with God, that we can recognize our own strength.

When we are strong and know we are walking the path of fulfillment, then it is easiest to reach out and offer a hand to one who is falling or stumbling. You realize that all there is, is in and of the Father. There are no exceptions. He is everywhere on this earth: in the sunset, in the blowing wind, in the rain that slashes through the storm. He is in the corner of your room. He is everywhere. Knowing this, erase fear from your mind, soul, and spirit. Let His great love fill your soul and reward you. Let Him take your hand and say, *"I love You, too. I recognize You, too, Father, for You are me and I am You. Thank You."*

Love is the strongest energy builder mankind possesses. It is only when man lacks love that he loses all faith in himself and in mankind, and experiences a loss of energy. Love is the most precious commodity mankind has during his period of living on this earth plane. The love of love is a *Universal Law* available to all of us. Man can reach into the "Pot of Love" and take for himself the exact amount of love that he needs.

Prior to our existing or living on this earth, we as spirits had a supply of love so great that the quantity and quality of that supply is unknown on the earth plane today. So when we are reincarnated, it bothers us to gather close to our fellow man, for we feel no warmth from him. Very often in his reincarnation, man goes through a period of forgetfulness and ceases to be warm and loving as he once was.

Deluge your life with love. That is the secret of successful living. Love all the people you meet, knowing that every man is a link in the chain of existence in your life. Some time in this lifetime on earth, he will serve in the divine plan of your life. Love all whom you meet, and accept their love. Do not doubt their love. We sometimes find ourselves doubting the love offered, asking ourselves, "How shall I accept this love? Do I need this much to subsist here on earth?" And then we wonder at the quality of the love offered and the purpose for which love is offered. Thus we build up a wall of doubt about the love extended or offered to us.

On this side of the curtain, it is natural for all men to love one another in great abundance. We can reach into the pocket of love offered, or we can engulf ourselves with self pity and lose the great love. The choice is ours. The man who chooses love is granted a peaceful coexistence with others and harmony rules his life. Here on earth, distrust of others awakens in us distrust of ourselves. It also makes us question, "Who am I? What am I? Do I deserve this trust and love?"

The Father commands us to live in true balance and harmony. How often do you find yourself disparaging yourself and others? Do you feel unhealthy, unwanted, unloved, and unhappy? Well, the key to all this is your own distrust of yourself and your fellow man. When you try to trust all of mankind, try sincerely to love all. A harmony exists within your life that will be the envy of others who live in an atmosphere of suspicion brought on by this distrust.

Equality is one of the *Universal Laws* probably only second to love. The Father accepts us all as equal. We must learn to accept those around us as equal to ourselves so that we do not allow disparaging words to create disharmony.

"I will not allow that to bother me. I will accede to God's wishes and be content. I will live in harmony with those around me, however simpler it might be to live in disharmony."

Always accede to God's wishes. "Thy will be done." In so doing, we allow Him to enter our minds and leave the firm impressions of His love upon us. Without His love, life has no meaning. We are blessed with the ability to see, to feel, and to smell; for as we abide with these laws, He brings harmony to us all. If we abide with the *Universal Laws*, we bring peace and harmony into our lives as well for all of mankind.

Think these thoughts through completely. Love is the most precious commodity in life. Without love, there can be no life. Whether it be the love of God, the love of parents, mates, or friends, love is a necessary ingredient. Love is a nourishment for the body, for the spirit, for the soul!

Love Ye One Another

I have been directed to communicate that the number one commandment of the Father is that of the title above.

"*Love Ye One Another*." Is it difficult to understand

this truth, for few respect one another--and if that be so, how then can they respect animals? Let all men know the Lord loves us all and that He exists within us all. All that He asks from us is to bless Him.

By communicating with Him, we rise to holier thoughts. We reach the heights of understanding, so that we are able to understand all of life more fully.

Rehearse within your mind the words you might say to a person cursing the Lord. "What has the Lord done unto thee that you take His name in vain?" Rehearse in your mind what you will say to the person abusing an animal, for are not animals loved and created by God also? Rehearse your words! Sound off! Be heard! Let people know your existence is not in vain.

We are all equal before the Lord. The lowly sparrow is equal even as the mighty whale. All are created by God. We should not feel any difference within our minds between each other. There can be no difference between humankind, be they rich or poor, peasant or royalty, illiterate or educated. All are equal in the sight of the Lord.

Harm no man. Instead, try to assist him in any way possible. Man knows how to hurt, but knows not how to ease the hurt. Acquaint yourself with the heart and soul of the Lord; so shall you know the heart and soul of the man.

The reversal of time and deeds is possible only when man understands in full these teachings. The Heavenly Father says, *"Come unto me and change your thinking about your fellow man; else hell on earth will be your reward."* The Father has heard the untruths spoken and His name used in vain, and the Father is angry. He does not and will not accept injustice, abuses done unto His children. Therefore, abuse no one, nor let anyone abuse you by using the name of God in vain.

Love Mercy

On taking office, former President Carter used the words from Micah in his acceptance speech: "What doth the Lord require of me but to do justly and to love mercy and kindness and to walk humbly with my God?"

Let us hope that man will henceforth truly live with these thoughts in his heart and soul.

All men are created equal. It is for each person his responsibility--what he makes of himself. Remember I have told you before that to evolve to a higher state a man must learn how to hold his head high and thank the Lord for every instance of his success. For the Lord is alive, and lives close to us. We must always control our anger, hold it in check; we must reject envy of others. Here the anointed ones begin to understand that to hold their heads high, they must remember to be humble--truly humble. Since we all originated from the same source, the same principles should guide our lives. It is the manner in which we accept our fate, our destiny, that distinguishes us one from another.

Are we remiss in our obligations to one another? If this is true, are we truly close to one another? Do we ever think of a soul other than ourselves? Are we selfish, lacking understanding of others? In time, therefore, we must be reborn to unlearn this selfishness, for the mercy of the Lord rests within our hands. He absolves us only when we understand that mercy is the most important aspect of our behavior. To have mercy for others and deplore injustice means we have found our way safely back home to the Father.

Again, what doth the Lord expect of us but to be humble, love mercy and have mercy, love justice for all, and walk humbly in the pathway of the Lord.

Dimension

The Father wants us to live together. He did not mean for us to hide away in some secluded spot and live alone. No man learns anything by separating himself from other members of society. This lesson may be difficult for the affluent man to learn: that he has a lesson to learn from someone less affluent or less educated than himself. For it has been said the Father said, "I love all of my children equally."

God wants us to acknowledge His presence within us, to know that that union lives on forever. Although man may find it difficult to live together with other men (he may seek to create disharmony, seek to annihilate others), he still must live with others.

Because the Father insists that we live together to understand the Father's thinking, He created us hoping we could and would live in a peaceful coexistence. That is the dimension He envisioned for mankind. He envisioned us as links in a chain, one link adding strength to the other; a complete chain of loving people living in true harmony, listening and practicing His laws.

We who live in the light of the Father must try to fulfill this dimension by reaching out to those who live in disharmony and adding our energy to theirs, thus establishing a precedent to evenness and equality. If we can add one thought, give one smile, assuage one pain, then we have succeeded in adding strength to the chain that the Father created.

Try--in your homes, in the homes of friends--to create a peaceful harmony among its members. Use your life as an example of what the Father envisioned when He created the chain, and that peaceful dimension that He yearns for His children.

He wants us to live a harmonious life, feeling no ill will toward any soul because of creed, color, or appearance. It is true we all feel closer to those who share our thoughts and beliefs, but we must try to feel close to all of mankind. It was one of the tenets of the covenant that we made with the Father before birth: *"Love Ye One Another."*

CHAPTER 4

FEAR

Fear Is an Illness

This is a meditative prayer to be said each night for one month before you lay your body down to rest for the night:

"I see tremendous colored balloons filled with helium. These balloons are carrying all of my troubles, all of my frustrations, all of my heartache up and away. These balloons float higher and higher away from me until the sky is a clear blue. Now, I am free and have no fears."

We must educate ourselves to think along these lines each evening before releasing our spirit to the Father. The Father works to cleanse the mind of all ill-conceived thoughts during this period of time. Enter into blissfulness with the Father, allowing your body, soul, and spirit to rest with Him.

Love is the demonstration of the Lord's way of life. That is the way He meant mankind to live--with love of oneself and for all of mankind. To preserve life and to elevate the quality of life is to rid one's mind of illness. When we understand how to rid our minds of illness, we begin to understand how the Father meant us to live.

The most pressing problem for mankind is to learn how to get rid of fear. Fear is the devastation felt and seen among men. Fear is what causes illness, for it places the complete body, the psyche, into disarray, setting loose forces within the psyche or mind of mankind known as "psychosomatic illness."

We must look ahead without fear, having deep faith. The Father observes the cause of the unrest within us and He sets up guards to diffuse the problems. We should have faith and try to understand His teachings, the teachings of truth. Fruit comes to those who believe;

fruit comes to those who try to help themselves by exploring their own mind, by stimulating the Lord's mind within themselves.

Diffuse your troubles by believing first in the Father, second in His obstinacy to treat all men equally. He tries so hard to diffuse and rid your mind of troubles. He tries to lead us and get us back on the pathway of life again, once we stumble and fall. We must listen very intently to His thoughts. He is diffusing our thinking with thoughts of love, and He fills our lives with understanding of how to help ourselves. We must learn to listen more intently and follow His guidance. <u>There is no illness on earth created by the Father</u>!

The individual inflicts punishment upon his own body by ill-conceived thoughts because of frustrations, because of things he wants to obtain--things he thinks he cannot bring to fruition. Once we establish the cause of our frustration, it is very easy to rid ourselves of it by facing it frontally and listening to the Father for the cure. It is all there, instant relief, because we can rid our minds of all ill-conceived thoughts.

Every man can change his complete life around if he will but listen, work for a change, and have faith that with the Father's help, it can be accomplished.

LIFE IS LOVE.
WITHOUT LOVE, THERE IS NO REAL LIVING.
LOVE IS LIFE WITHOUT FEAR.

Affirmation: Say to yourself, *"I will live close to the Father daily. I will sense His will. I will sense His thinking. Trouble cannot come into my life as long as the Father assures me of this truth, for then I can assure myself of a happy life without fear. My life shall be an example among mankind. No harm can come into my life. He lives close to me, to show me the way out of all my troubles. I evince no fear, for the Lord watches over me."*

How to Get Rid of Fear

Destiny

The mind is your destiny. Within your mind lies everything that you are, everything that you can be, everything that you have been. What you make of it is where you're going and what you're going to be.

Fulfillment

You are striving for fulfillment--destiny. To achieve it, you must find the Father. You must first ask yourself how to find that fulfillment, for that alone brings happiness, health for yourself, and the ability to help others around you.

The Father

What do you feel when you do not live close to the Father? Or when you do not accept Him into your life as a partner? Uneasiness, uncertainty, and unhappiness.

The soul cries out for accord, peace, unity, and acceptance. Do you want to live with the negatives or the opposite, the positives? The choice is up to you. Each of us has a choice, free will. When you find the Father, He gives the greatest gifts. Light! Love!

We are but energy, offered to us by God's grace. Without the light, we cannot live. We don't look favorably upon early retirement from work or from life itself, because then we lose our energy or we don't use it correctly. Mankind seems to want to give up on life as soon as he comes up against an area that he cannot accept or solve. The early retirements mentioned above seem to affect the brain and destroy man's energy flow. Once he accepts retirement, he ceases to search, struggle, and use his mind and knowledge. This causes the loss of energy and light. He destroys his own energy flow and, in essence, accepts death.

Passing Through the Door

Man has strange concepts as to what occurs toward

the end of life. We have been assured time and time again by our masters and teachers that no one dies in agony--that there is no pain in actual death itself. It is as simple as passing through one door and entering another room. Those who have the ability to see auras can see the spirit of the deceased standing to one side and waiting for its signal or time to leave. Each person has a silver cord leading from the solar plexus that somehow is attached to the aura, and at the moment of death the cord is severed and the aura floats away. The silver cord is the light and energy that attaches us to the Father. It is, therefore, that which is designated as the link to the God within us. After the aura has floated away at the moment of death, the spirit is then greeted by the loved ones who have preceded them. There is the sound of beautiful music and laughter and joy, for it is a period of reunion, not only for those that have been with us in this particular lifetime, but for many lifetimes in the past.

   As you can see, there is no need for fear. Try to practice and believe in love; that is the most important thing in life. Love is the most precious gift mankind can give and accept. For God is love.

CHAPTER 5

KARMA

We Cannot Live Others' Lives Nor Take on Their Problems

We must have sympathy for all of mankind in times of distress. However, there is a demarcation point between sympathy and assuming the burden of another's troubles. However, if by helping or assuming another's troubles you are helping your friend escape from his responsibilities, you thereby include his troubles into your own life, thus excluding him from fulfilling his destiny and learning his lessons. What is gained by this? What does your friend gain? Nothing! You lose much of the energy you should be using in a positive manner to help others who are truly in need of your help. You then take from your friend his ability to solve his own troubles or problems. You are asking God to mask His face from your friend.

What does this mean? We only learn through doing, through living. Each man has his own signal; each has his own role to perform, his own lessons to learn during this time on earth. When you lose or use up the energy that was originally generated for your use, who then will help you face the problems you yet have to conquer in your lifetime? A supply of energy is always available to those who need, to regenerate their own energy if they have used their energy wisely and aided others correctly by helping them think so that they can work out their own problems. Equal time to equal energy. In other words, if you use up your energy displaying emotion and temperament, using it unwisely, how then can you recoup that lost energy? Who, then, are you helping? No one.

That is the message of truth we are aiming to get across. Access to that energy supply is readily available to all of mankind equally. Why isn't it distributed equally? Because somewhere along the line we have wasted the original supply, either in some other lifetime or by not using our energy wisely in order to manifest or finish our destiny in the time allotted. How then can we equate this thought with gathering energy already used and that which remains above us, but still available? That is the point in question.

We must gather energy positively by helping to solve our own troubles, while giving others communications of truth and guidance--thus instructing them how to go about solving their own troubles, but not doing it for them. Allow them time to use the energy and the advice you have given to them. If it is not disbursed or used correctly--as it was meant to be used--then they have not heeded your advice and must accept the consequences themselves. Once the teacher gives the lesson, it is no longer his karma or responsibility if the student does not learn or heed the lesson.

Parents often advise their children from their own past experiences, only to find it all a waste of energy. Painful as it may be, you cannot, according to the original teachings of truth, use your past experiences or add your energy to solving their problems. You can only be assured of rapid growth by solving your own problems and allowing others to solve theirs. In other words, if we allow others to dispose of or solve their own problems after we once advise them, and we solve our own problems, we both grow, learn, and add more knowledge toward the purpose of our lives.

Our karma belongs to us. Their karma belongs to them. When we once truly learn this bit of knowledge, it then becomes wisdom.

Why Inherit Karma?

There is little peace in the world. All is confusion,

intrigue, and smart maneuvering; we need more godliness and kindness in our own immediate environment. If each and every man would make a pledge to do his part of enlightening each prejudiced word or action, all could be delivered from this dreaded fungus--prejudice and discrimination. We are but one single unit. But many single units united make their impression felt. We must again feel the love and compassion of one man for another.

We were put here to work as a community, not as a single person. All that we were sent was meant to be used as men united in one duty--that is, living through God. It is only when we segregate ourselves, living apart in little islands, that we grow so far inward that we no longer see that the stranger is a whole man too, with the same loneliness, same loves, same honors as our own.

Get to know other men of different faiths, races, and colors, if it is just to keep an open mind when you encounter them in the daily task of living. Bless this man in your heart; ask to see him as God sees him. Consciously done, it cannot fail but to open up a new gentleness and graciousness to all peoples. This is very true in all phases of living. We do not say, when at war, that we will only take the "certain" people of this nation. No, all come to defend a beloved country. All men at that time can learn to live at peace with themselves and their fellow men. If this be so, why then can't we give up the ego-building of subjugating other men?

Ridicule, prejudice, hatred, and intolerance are the tools a man employs to build his own self-esteem. But these things only make him feel repulsion with himself because fundamentally we are all God's creations, and no matter what we choose to put on as garments, our inner core is God. We never lose it. No one ever does, and that is why it is so easy for a man to be a confessed sinner one minute and a religious zealot the next. This transformation can come about at any time, so don't feel free to judge or criticize any man. Although he is stumbling along the wrong paths in utter darkness, he may take the right road at any time. He is never lost-- never beyond God's help.

Newspapers should carry articles that definitely name prejudice and intolerance for what it is--name it, proclaim it as they would a dreaded disease.

It has become very smart to be rude, to hurry, to rush, to laugh at all attempts at goodness and gentleness. We are a people shackled in fear of ridicule. We must, each and every one of us, break off from the stagnant jungle growth of a decayed civilization--break off and be reborn again in the plant of God's love.

All through the ages men had to be reborn. That is God's part in the scheme of things. We get so far from the rays of our Father's light that we start feeling ourselves lost, and we feel the lack of His warmth and growing power. It is then we must again return and bask in His radiation. So it is; we have gone so far that we are now in a wasteland--a desert of living, so to speak-- where we cannot exist. We must drink the waters of His eternal truth, eat the bread of humility, kindness, and love. Then and only then can we start rebuilding a people ravaged by selfishness, materialism, and self-seeking gratification.

Every unselfish act, every kind word, is a step in the right direction. This is a slow process; inch by inch we progress in God's work. Once out of the darkness, we will find a new world of abundant living.

There is not one man who lives on this earth who can truthfully say, "I am better than my neighbor." We are all equal in the eyes of God. It is simply this: we are all evolving in our own particular pattern that God made for us, and we find if the subject be pursued that we are all ignorant, but only about different things. This illustration proves a point:

A great financier who had made a huge fortune decided that he would indulge his ambition to go hunt big game. He felt that it would add to his prestige at his local club if he, too, could brag of his expeditions and trophies. He had the smartest shop outfit him for his journey; he left nothing to chance. After three months of a tiring journey, he came at last to the campsite. He had wired ahead for the best guide in that section of the country. The next morning he was ready to be off on his adventure. He was shocked and appalled at the sight of his guide, whom the local interpreter assured him was the best guide in the business. He looked with disgust at a gnarled old man in tattered clothes and an ill-kept beard. He said to the man who was the go-between, "Surely you don't expect me to go off into the jungle with this creature? I'll probably be murdered my first night out!" The answer he got was, "You will see, Sahib, you will see."

With great misgivings he took to the jungle on the back of a trusty Jeep. The guide talked little, except a word of caution now and then. The beaters took up the rest of this procession.

Once in the hunting grounds, more and more the great man began to see his own inadequacies and depend more and more on his wise guide. More than once, an ill-spent bullet that did not find its mark had to be corrected by the expert shot of the guide.

On the way back to the camping grounds, the great man very humbly thanked the old guide, saying, "You saved my life." The old man's only reply was an ill-disguised look of disgust.

When it was time to leave, he commented to the interpreter of the great ability and skill of the guide. The interpreter, in turn, told him, "You think better now of the man who presented his services to you, Sahib?" He also told the interpreter if he ever came back again he would certainly want the same guide at his side. The interpreter spoke, saying, "I'm afraid not, Sahib. He, your guide, will not lay down his life again for such a small man. You see, Sahib, although you are a great one on the other side of the world, you are a bad hunter here. But, of course, Sahib, who can be wise in all things?"

Karma- 58

CHAPTER 6

FAITH

Divinity: How God Works the Tapestry of Life

Live for today and enjoy each moment of today, this very day. Do not look forward to what can be done tomorrow; only live today. Do not borrow trouble by anticipating or looking ahead and worrying about what will happen when you grow old and feeble. Think of today, of preparing the tapestry of life today, and do it to the best of your ability. Let tomorrow take care of itself If you but have faith in this one lesson to learn, you will make life so much easier and happier to live. Doubt not God; He directs all things and it is His plan that today we enjoy each moment. Believe and He will direct us tomorrow. So learn this one lesson: enjoy today and worry not, for all of God's children will be led back tomorrow to follow the pathway back home to the Lord.

He directs all patterns. One is different from the other, for each of us has lessons we must learn that must be accomplished here on earth. Therefore, now you understand the difference in people. What one can accomplish, another cannot; but that does not make him less a chosen child of God. No, it is only that he is directed another way to do another thing in God's timing. We must do all that He has created for us to do. Be creative within yourself and seek His pathway. Follow His pattern that He has helped you design on your tapestry.

Doubt not His direction, for it may take you to many foreign and strange places, but He directs you always back to the singular pattern He has outlined for you to follow. Doubt not His words or wisdom when He directs you to do this work. He has designed a beautiful and wondrous pattern in your tapestry for you to follow.

Confusion and Its Lesser Evils

We can all be made complete through prayer. In the beginning, men were so engrossed in daily survival--just meeting bodily needs--that confusion seeped in. Confusion is heir of the modern era. With more free time on our hands and more of our material wants gratified, we are nevertheless a very frustrated people. The more we obtain, the more we need; the more we need, the greater the pressure. We seem to walk an endless treadmill of frustration. The only solution is to put our trust in the hands of God. Let His wisdom guide us through the maze of modern living. Let His laws of supply and demand be balanced. There are three basic hungers: physical, spiritual, and sexual. We exist only by gratifying all three.

The first and foremost are the needs of the soul. We may feed the body, take care of its needs, but deny it the supreme pleasure of listening to the heavenly music;

therein lies frustration. Add material gains to all the gastric and sexual pleasures, and we still find ourselves beset by fears, suffering loneliness deep as a chasm. The more we trade in the counterfeit coin of materialism, the more material things we need. It is indeed a fool's gold we dig! We strive mightily; then we sell all on the exchange of materialism. We claw our way to the top, only to find that what we have gained glitters for a few minutes and goes out like the flame of a flickering penny candle. Ignore the spiritual, and the mind immediately sets up a standard of "escapes" to lull its soul's ache for gratification.

We spend endless years trying desperately to achieve security, wealth, property, power. We frantically add to our pile of trash. If we have five thousand dollars in the bank, we feel safe only momentarily. We soon find that to be really safe, we need ten thousand dollars--and so it goes on and on.

All we must do is turn to God with the thought, *"I am Your child. Keep me this day!"*

He will send whatever you need for that particular day. All your needs will be answered. You will learn by daily practice how to face a greedy world with tranquility and serenity. We know we exist in the shadow of a bountiful Master who provides all we need for our spiritual welfare.

Just relax and surrender to Him. Stop straining; listen to His soothing tones. We can only learn to float in water by relaxing; when we struggle and fear the water, we sink below the surface. Relax, lie calm on the water of life, and float. So it is with God. Come to God as a little child, trusting in His kindness to provide for the very much-loved child.

Take God In As a Partner

"The God in me can accomplish and overcome whatsoever I may face today!" (You can succeed in anything you try.)

Banish evil thoughts about others. The Lord blessed us with this truth tonight. He recounted how we talked with Him once upon a time when He told us, "Go, seek your fortune alone. Set out alone and see how long it takes you to find your way safely back home to me."

We wandered along the road of life without His help, without His smile, without even the daily visitations we had grown accustomed to. Then, when upon a course set by the wind, we had wandered off the shores of Greece. There we stood up and saw the sea walls for the first time. Then we knew we had found civilization. We wandered through the streets of Greece wondering. Did the Lord know we had landed our craft safely? Was He watching? We had grown bored with our lives together with Him. He was always telling us how to think, what to think, how to live! Now we were alone, absolutely alone. He, the Father, knew the truth: that we were wasting our lives alone, and until He motivated us further we would be lost, ambling along life's pathway alone, aimlessly waiting for the time to die again. Then we knew the truth that once again we had to hold foremost in our minds the thought that we were indeed His true children; that indeed He did not despise us--that He had never left us alone, but we indeed had deserted Him. In total truth, has not mankind done so today? How many men set their goals ahead of time and then set the record straight with the Lord? Do they ask His permission to set their sails? According to recorded history, has man ever amounted to a crabapple without a partnership with the Lord? Man has but to raise his head up high and say to the Father, *"Take me back safely, Father. Teach me the rudiments of truth. Allow me to follow the pathway we have set for ourselves with Your blessings, Father!"* Always with His blessings and permission. If you suit only yourself, what you hate in others is destined to become part of your life unless you can change your thinking.

Thus the lesson to learn: *"Harvest no negative thoughts about others. Let each live his life as he sees fit. If he asks for help, help him, but not without his request, and always remember, Thy <u>will be done.</u> <u>Father.</u>"*

Give your life to the Father; surrender it unto His keeping. He can do a lot more with it than you can, laboring alone. You can flow with His grace and let each day be an adventure in living, or you can shackle your legs with the chains of disbelief, disgust, and boredom. We all see people who are actually serving sentences of living. They look back with contempt on their yesterdays, expect nothing of today, and fear all the tomorrows. What a pitiful sight! Here is man, who could bathe in God's holy light and soar like a great bird, plodding along with the weight of godlessness and indifference upon his shoulders.

We are living a great indifference, day in and day out. Our very attitude of, "I don't care" is our defeat. We must start caring, living, trying, and we will then have the problem half won. It's going to take people with great faith and more courage to live and restore the "mess of misguided men" we have living in this world.

We must learn to live constructively. Once we start beaming success in our lives, we will be successes. *"As a man thinketh, so he is."*

Try thinking in big terms; soon we find it will attract all to us. This isn't meant to sound like a miracle worker, but step by step we will be pulling ourselves out of the lethargy that besets us. Prayer alone works little miracles, but prayer combined with definite effort and realistic work on our part really does work wonderful changes in all lives. Once we try this formula, we will find that we have a way of life that will enable us to accomplish more and more.

Take God in as your partner. Give in <u>His</u> name some definite amount to pay--your share, so to speak--of the upkeep of a successful endeavor. All given in His name is indeed blessed. He knows that man existing alone, solely for his own indulgence, is a sad creature. We are expected in God's scheme of things to help our families, but He definitely stipulated neighbors, also. So in the true sense of the word, He meant all people needing help. He knew that in doing good deeds we do ourselves more good than the recipient. He knew it acted as a tonic on our inner selves.

Once we start living outside ourselves, we have found the answer to happier lives.

A Time to Think and Co-exist With Mankind

There comes a time when we have to limit ourselves. There is a time to live, a time to laugh, and a time to think things through. You effect a reconciliation between yourself and the Father each time you come into contact with Him.

The Lord, blessed be He, is in our midst at all times. There is never a moment or thought that does not originally belong to Him alone. Without Him, there is no existence. Utter confusion reigns today because mankind has lost contact with the Lord.

Accept Him; take Him in as a partner in all things. Vow to help all of mankind by accomplishing that which you set out to do.

In the beginning when men were created, they lived the truth alongside of other men who lived the same way. They fashioned their lives in accord with the Father's wishes and acquiesced to His desires. Yet today, they are the same men and women who wandered over the centuries. Why has mankind become so complacent that they have forgotten the Father?

Why don't people continue to believe in Him? What has happened that mankind should change so completely? The effect has been complete disillusionment! Negativity is rampant and causes indigestion, cancer, other illness, as well as the horrible illusions and visions of despair that we experience.

There is a breakdown of contemporary society. The richest of people live in vain, not knowing how to use their wealth to achieve happiness and fulfillment.

The absolution of mankind depends upon recognition of the Father. Without Him, there is nothing man can accomplish in this lifetime. There is little man can do to fulfill his destiny. Negativity now accompanies man; thus he accomplishes nothing in this lifetime and even less when transferred to another planet or thought influence.

Radical thoughts bring him closer to negativity, while the calming technique that the Lord uses is lost upon him.

Condemn him not. Negativity is rampant within mankind's mind. There is no negativity that he can withstand as long as he feels about his world as he does. Encourage men to seek higher lives. Living among mankind is not easy. There are always those who accede to their own wishes, caring not for others. But you must withstand these thought waves and succeed by loving all of mankind and by saying, "They can't help these faults."

Until a different trend is felt among mankind, negativity will remain. It is up to man to live among his own, regardless of prejudices. He has to face himself, he has to succeed regardless of conditions; it is up to the individual. You must maintain your equilibrium regardless of how you feel. Accede only to the Lord's wishes. His majesty succeeds or supersedes over all of mankind. He does not annoy anyone. He is ever-present among us and helps us to succeed if we listen and hear what He is talking about. Allow Him the freedom among your thoughts and accede to His wishes by carrying out the fulfillment meant for us all for this lifetime. This planet earth has many revolutions per minute; yet it accedes to the wishes of the Lord or it would not still be turning upon its axis. So determine to set your mind free from trouble and accede to His wishes.

To Understand and Recognize the Father

God equates truth for all of mankind even unto the end of time. He asserts that His will be done. He declares truth for all of mankind. He equates evil for all of mankind, too.

The evil spirit within us is dominant; we have to

muster the courage to cleanse it from our brains, our minds. Otherwise, the example of truth will never be understood. Fortunately, you have heard this statement, this affirmation of *truth everlasting*. Mankind must understand how necessary it is for him to know this *truth*. The Father continues to wait for the obvious understanding among His children. He waits for recognition. Yes, the Father waits to be recognized by His family of children.

If this dissertation is viewed by all of mankind today, how few would believe it existed or that the Father existed at all? Others would say it never happened, just as they are now saying the exodus from Egypt never took place, that extermination of man never takes place. While the mercy of the Lord awaits all of us, we never listen carefully enough to understand His truths, even today.

The dissertations He would like to bring, the education He would like to leave with His children, forever will be lost until mankind admits His existence within their lives.

Trouble

"I am God's child; no harm can come to me."

Equate trouble with purpose in life. Without troubles, we would not enjoy our lives, nor would we be able to live life to the fullest. We would not fulfill our destiny, nor would we achieve the height of evolution were we not tempered by our misfortunes. It hastens our growth. We do not fully understand life, so we do not understand why troubles are necessary.

When trouble strikes, we must fight and work our way back to the top. Take time and work hard to understand this lesson of *truth* for it is many-pronged, many-faceted.

The way of life remains equally as long for the Father as it does for us who live on earth. Please understand what is happening: any trouble for you is trouble for us all. The end result adds up to the evidence that God remains living and we must entrust our lives into His hands and His warmth, knowing full well He trusts us, too, with His life; for are we not all of us, one unto one?

All that the Father asks of us is that we live close to Him, that we raise our faces to His each morning upon arising and say, *"Here I am, Father, take me back home to Thee anew."*

Yes, if each morning we perform this simple task, our purpose in life will be rewarded by His presence in us, and the renewal of life daily. The troubles, the lessons that we must learn, will be easier to bear, knowing that our evolution is the prize we are rewarded with until the end of time.

If we but understand there is a reason for everything happening--that there is a well-organized universe--it will make our trials and tribulations easier to bear.

Judge Not, Lest Ye Be Judged

Do you understand how to think deeply? How to meditate correctly? Ask the Lord to grant you the wisdom to understand how to achieve both, as well as your total fulfillment. Do not allow others to upset you. Say, *"I forgive those who would harm me, and I will not allow myself to think upon them."* Yes, this is a way to negate the poison that builds up within your minds and hearts against those who seek to harm, hurt, or distress you. Look for the brighter, positive side of life. Do not allow negativity to enter your consciousness. Say, *"No, I reject your negative vibrations. I pray for your salvation but I do not allow you to distress me further."* Say,

"Please, God, forgive that man for trying to make my life miserable. Allow me to forgive and forget." Soon that positive thinking will heal you and you will be able to solve the conflict.

Say, *"I love Thee; I salute Thee, Lord,"* for each man is indeed the Lord, for the Lord lives within each man. There is no devil. All mankind belongs to the Lord. Keep this thought uppermost and repeat it many times every day. Raise yourself up to the highest abode, and accept the blessings of the Father.

He sends thoughts of love, of plenty and sufficiency needed to exist here on this earth plane. If you have not that which you desire, perhaps it was meant to be so. Surely He will send to you that which you need, not necessarily what you think you want. There is a big difference. There will always be enough for you to exist upon this earth.

It is a matter of energy exchange, exchange of energy with Him. Say, *"Take me safely home to Thee, Father, and exchange energy with me so that I may exist in peace with good health and happiness and an abundance of what I need, that I may fulfill my lifetime here on the earth plane."*

The Lord will accept you even if you do not finish the covenant that you made with Him this time around. If your energy supply runs out, He will never reprimand you. He will always tell you how well you have done, for He loves you and he will tell you what you have accomplished. He will also tell you that you must return to fulfill that which has not been completed.

Thus, my friends, we return time and time again, some day to finish completely the covenant we pledged to fulfill long ago.

Equality

The quality of thinking is most important. What that means is if you think things through carefully with a great deal of effort, you are able to go deeper and accept more idea-provoking thoughts. If you accept by rote the thoughts of others without question, or the directions given by others, actually the impression in your mind will be lessened.

The ideas brought to you through the deep thinking process open the doors of your mind, and you will be amazed how easily you can accept new ideas and understand them fully. The Father makes available equal messages to all of His children. Whether or not we receive these messages depends upon our level of evolvement. We all started out together, but some of us evolved to a higher level. It is a matter of training ourselves to understand His thoughts.

Fear responds to fear. If you are fearful of accomplishing a task, or if you say to yourself, "I can never understand these thoughts, therefore why try?" you set into motion negativity which is a thoughtwave of fear. You close the door to the universal energy available to all of us. You're saying, "I am afraid. I have great doubts." Use a positive attitude. Direct your mind to a fresh idea, saying, *"I can. I will. I know."* Then you will find that you can accomplish what you strive to do. This is true for every event, for every deed in your life.

JUDGE NOT. One of the basic *Universal Laws*, the one most often abused, is: Judge yourself, as you would have others judge you. Truthful people judge themselves much more harshly.

Equality is the theme of this lesson. If you feel equal to a task, you can accomplish it. You set into motion an attitude, a thoughtwave that creates the energy needed to finish or accomplish this task. For this reason, you must try to visualize your needs. The Father wants you to accomplish what you set out to do, to have what you need for peace of mind, to make your life happy, contented, and fulfilled. Visualize your life as complete with all your needs fulfilled. In this manner you set into motion the energy necessary to bring this harmony and peace into your life. This is a divine law of truth. If you fear, you set fear into motion. You exude it from your mind. Beware of every thought! Try to make every thought positive. Try to equate your thoughts with love. Do not allow fear or hatred to splinter them. One example my students refer to constantly is so many people have fears that they will not have enough money upon retirement. If you permit this fear to constantly distort your thoughts, it will set into motion that which will make your fears come true. Instead, visualize and say: "I will have all the money I need as long as I live on this earth. I shall, in turn, give that which I do not need to those who are in need."

Yes, this is using *Universal Law* correctly; to think and set into motion positive thoughts that actually will happen later on. By this affirmation, by thinking and visualizing, you create the energy equal to your thought and there will be no <u>need</u> whatsoever in your lifetime on earth. Thoughts and creative ideas or other solutions are brought to you during your quiet time to show you how to create this security.

Approach problems with children positively. Say, "John and Mary will marry the right people so that they may fulfill their destiny. They will accept the right job or profession to help them fulfill their lifetimes."

That is all you can do in such instance. Propel your thoughts into the ether. What your child requires may be different in his or her mind than in yours. It is his destiny that he has to fulfill. You are merely saying,

"Your will be done, Father. Your will so that John and Mary may find their way safely back home to Thee."

One must claim that which belongs to him and nothing more. Claim only happiness, peace and contentment so that mind, soul, and the physical being can be in harmony. If you feel equal to a thought, it will continue to flower.

"Seek and ye shall find" is exactly the same thought in different words.

Ordained ministers may not always be men true to the Father. They may accelerate their own thinking. Too often educated men overlook the truthwaves that are deposited into their minds. They cannot fashion their lives with *truth*. They are educated, and so they must follow the line of reasoning they have been trained to accept. Not all educated men embody *truth*. Seek perhaps a pauper, an uneducated man. Seek the *truth* wherever it may be. He sees life in the raw as it really is, for he lives according to the creed, once fashioned after the *truth*, sent to earth to the early man. He has learned, *"Do unto others as you would have others do unto thee."*

The farmer has learned to do unto nature that which is right in order that he might harvest his crops. So we must harvest the wisdom and live.

CHAPTER 7

LIFE EVERLASTING

These thoughts have come to me through meditative thought waves, and the thoughts expressed in this book are not of this writer, but those dictated to me directly from a higher source. I have chosen to accept these words to be exact and truthful, so as to help find a way to eradicate fear and hopelessness from all mankind as has been revealed to me.

From within these passages you will find lessons to direct your thinking each day to help you overcome the fear of life and find fulfillment for all of those of you who will follow the pathways clearly marked upon the "signposts" in this manuscript. In accepting these facts, you will live a happier chosen life, for each of you has chosen the life you now lead.

Make Life Worthwhile

Your life is directed within your inner thoughts through the Divine Being of the Lord, but you are left with a choice. He always gives His children free will. To do His will is the simple way of winding around the roads of life, to reweave all of the loose ends of life's tapestry. Because each of you has re-embodied ideally for one thing and one thing only, and that is to dispel or rid yourself of karma you have incurred in another lifetime. Deal with these thoughts and deeds by casting them out of your life so you do not have to live again and again. You can accomplish all this by accepting the Lord as a partner in your life. We have tried to show you the best and easiest way to do these tasks that lie ahead for you, but it is up to you to decline or accept His partnership. If you accept and live according to the *Laws* of the Ten Commandments and in concert with Universal Law that has been decreed for all of mankind, animals and plant life alike, your life will be devoid of stress. But if you continue to live with your depressions and unforgiving heart among your fellow man, then your life will be lived in vain. Then again, at another time, you will ask to come back and relive this adventure.

Search Within Your Mind for Truth

"Almighty Lord, Father of the universe, we seek the wonderment and radiance of Your light for us all, so that we may dispense it among mankind."

We are taught that wisdom lies within man's mind, but negative forces drive it away. The wisdom of the sages of old waits to be reinstated. It is like a freezer full of food waiting to be emptied, one item at a time. Knowledge is seldom lost, yet during some periods of history mankind has refused to utilize his own energy, his own source of wisdom. Lest it be totally lost, we shall try to re-inform instead of misinform. *Truth everlasting* originated in the past; it is for us to evoke these truths. The wisdom we seek is harbored within us from long ago. Seek then within the chambers of your mind, for down deep within is to be found the Master's *truth*, together with the wisdom our higher selves ache to impart so that we may find the high road to *life everlasting.*

Wisdom lives within our minds, planted there centuries ago, foreshadowing our future. Yes, the future grows from the past. Seek the learning of the past. Seek it, search for it, re-establish it for all mankind. Observe, listen to different opinions, but do not take the refuge offered you by them. Seek only the higher answers; sift out the *truth* as chaff is sifted from wheat, and use it wisely. It has been said that evil lurks in all the hearts. The secret is to learn to weigh also the amount of *truth* lying dormant within the heart and have it outweigh the evil. Use it wisely. *Truth* remains alive within you to call upon at all times.

How to Find Life's Plan

"God, send me the power of believing and the proof of my convictions."

You can change your life and make it happy. We also have stated that this is accomplished with the use of basic *Universal Laws*. One must have a pattern for one's life, a map guiding us, giving us direction, indicating what we must accomplish. Such a map leads us along the path to fulfill our destiny. We must understand also that we are but energy created in the image of God. It is His energy that He has given to us that makes us the individuals we are, all of us "created in His image."

A life's plan is essential. What do we want to make of our lives? What goals do we hope to accomplish? How do we plan to accomplish these goals to fulfill our plan? Here again, faith is necessary. We must learn to direct the energy sources needed to help us accomplish our goal by using the Lord's light correctly. We must be positive in our thinking! *"I can do this. I want to do this; therefore with the Father's light, I can do this."*

Have faith; know that everything is possible. Banish fear from your heart, for fear clogs the energy force. When the first bit of doubt flickers, get rid of it with a positive assertion: *"He will help me. He will guide and direct me."*

Believe completely and you will soon see changes taking place. These changes will give you more respect for yourself. The people around you will begin to see the new you, the person of substance, the individual who knows where he is going and what he is doing. A new aura of success appears around you and soon, because of this positive attitude and the faith you have in yourself and the Father, wonderful things come into being for you.

This is easier to do than you may think. It's just a matter of practice. Again the old adage holds true: "Practice makes perfect." From morning until night, from waking time to sleep time, practice! Practice! Practice!

Everyone has moments of depression when he loses self-confidence in himself, in what he is doing. Retrace your steps and return to your first positive thoughts and assertions. You will then find yourself back to accomplishing your goals in life.

Make your plan worthwhile. Don't just say, "All I want to do is earn a million dollars." Arrange your plans architecturally to accomplish wonderful things in your lifetime--the wonderful things that will be stimulating in nature and will make you happy of heart. In so doing, the by-product may well be the million dollars. This will be the extra bonus for living close to the Father and having faith in His plan for you.

Life Is Not An Aimless Experience

Life is not an aimless wandering. Life is a fulfillment of tasks left undone in previous lifetimes. Some choose to return to help others in need of learning the wisdom lost centuries ago. Indeed, those blessed to return to earth in order to earn their degree of learning (unlearned in previous lifetimes) need to help themselves for their fulfillment. The most direct way is to cast their thoughts into the ether. Questions sent out before meditation or sleep often bring answers that we seek and need for fulfillment

Try this experiment before going to sleep: Ask pertinent questions about previous lifetimes and ask for complete recall upon awakening. After some practice, you will be aware of a divine light. Angels of mercy will present themselves to you during your meditation and sleeping time, and will give you the answers that you need. Record your thoughts the first thing in the morning. They may be the answers to your problems.

Each person has his own destiny. There are no aimless lives. You need to find the way to make daily living happy, joyous, and simple. This knowledge, in turn, must be shared with those with whom you live, those with whom you come in contact--with family and friends.

Remember, my children, if life ran smoothly all the time, it would have no meaning. We would learn nothing. Mankind has just begun to understand that if he had not created negativity he would not have to learn to overcome or cope with it. Thus we learn through persevering, through lessons learned. Remember (when you complain) that things weren't meant to run smoothly all the time. We learn by coping with problems on a day-to-day basis.

Each morning upon awakening, think good thoughts. *"This is going to be the best day of my life!"* Don't allow negativity to inhibit your mind. Instill happiness and you have treated yourself to the good life. If you envision good and happy thoughts, only good can exist! By existing in an atmosphere where light overshadows negativity, we follow the pathway that leads to the fulfilling of our destiny.

CHAPTER 8

VIBRATION

Energy

There is energy sufficient for everyone. Just reach up and ask for it. Lift your face to heaven and say, *"Teach me the truthful path to life everlasting. Award me happiness. Please hear me."*

The Lord is with us always. He rewards us with energy. Seek and ye shall find. Ask and it shall be given. Everyone is rewarded in a like manner. Institute this thinking in your group: *"Hear no evil, speak no evil, know no evil! Thus, live no evil!"*

Destiny forges ahead if we let it happen. If we recognize and allow our herald angels to act, they will renew our energy and our spirit. We know this to be the truth. The Master watches over us, guides and divines with us. He adjudicates this truth. Adverse thinking, He tells us, is never found in heaven. A disgruntled, dissatisfied, troubled man is seldom found in heaven. It is only on the earth plane that man feels dissatisfied. As soon as he meets his Master on his trip back home, the disgruntled, dissatisfied, troubled feelings leave him.

The Father, Master over all of us, furthers His study of human nature and reprimands us for using His energy unwisely when we accept despondency or illness, for nature meant us not to be solemn or ill. Destiny and nature punish us with negativity if we ask for and allow negativity, but when we wear the raiment of *Truth* and a smiling face, the Father rewards us with smiling *Truths.* He rewards us with energy to renew our lifetime on earth.

This reign on earth encompasses only a small amount of time. Use it wisely and welcome the *Truth* instilled within your mind each time your herald angels renew their faith and thoughts. Reward them by listening to them. Solemnity is not native to us; sadness is man-made. Reward yourself by smiling and being happy every moment of your life. Reward them, too, by trying to be happy each moment of your life.

Illness belongs to the dead, not to the living. Tell your students not to accept illness. This *truth*, this *law*, lives on and on into eternity. If you accept this *truth*, illness will not cling to you. If you say, *"Here on earth I am happy, I salute the Lord Himself for His mercy shines down upon this earth plane for us all."* He instills these thoughts into our minds and, while negativity may surround us, it dare not touch us. With the radiance of His smile and the raiment's of His *truth*, God showers us with joy and happiness.

Sincerity is the most precious gift one human being has to offer another. If without sincerity in our thinking and actions, the Lord rewards us with situations whereby we learn lessons of truthfulness. We reap what we sow. If we want an active life, free of illness, we must live it! Condemn no man; simply allow him his way of life. Reward yourself. Reward yourself by refusing to accept an assault upon your name. Sometimes men distrust true believers--hate and envy them. Ignore such men. Salute the Lord and cleanse your own breast of hatred and envy. Say, *"I hate no man. I permit everyone his freedom, but I ignore deceitful people!"* Stay away; do not come into the presence of such people, for by your presence, their poison and hatred only festers anew.

Light and Energy

All energy begins with the Lord. Yes, the energy source commences with the Lord's light. Historically, all men depend on the Lord's light from the beginning of time, because without it we cease to exist.

We gather energy through the Lord's light; He lives

within us. We must always remember we are one with God. It will make our lives easier to live if we understand and feel that the Father is always close within us. Without His energy that causes us to function as human beings, we will cease to exist. In order to continue the energy source given to us by the Lord's light, we have to think our thoughts through and educate ourselves.

As an example, we have just noted that our energy source or light comes from the Father. We should ponder this and see what refreshing answers we can come up with to substantiate this statement. One of the Universal Laws states, *"If we think positively we receive positive answers, but if we think, live, and breathe negativity, only negative things come into our lives."*

Therefore, if we think positive thoughts and gain the positive attitude, we gain positive momentum which adds to our light or energy. We don't deplete our energy in the positive state of mind as we do when we are thinking and living negatively.

The Father equates thoughts with light. Therefore, if we speak, live, and feel positive, we attract positive light. Negativity brings dark, unfulfilling gloom and a depletion of our energy.

The energy source remains ever the Father's. We can add to our own supply in order to attain the highest evolution, that which all men seek so as to fulfill the destiny for which he originally came to earth.

It is said one of the first basic Universal Laws was given: *"Love each other; love all of mankind."*

What is love but a positive energy? Give love and you receive love. Send out hatred and it comes back to you.

This is a basic example of living positively (love)--of living negatively (hate). Remember, love. You have heard it so much, but prove to yourself that the law works. Choose some person you don't particularly care for. Start sending thoughts of love to him regularly every morning upon awakening and every evening before falling to sleep--whenever your mind is free.

You will soon see different reactions from that person. You will begin to see qualities you had overlooked or not noticed before. Prove to yourself love does work, and you will gain positive energy to add to your supply so that you may be fulfilled in this lifetime on earth.

Face Life Frontally

Today we read the truth from the book of knowledge that told us to face life unafraid, not to evade the issues that confront us. Even the ancient Hebrews knew this to be true: Face life frontally--do not evade the issues of *truth everlasting*. The masters who guard us knew that even the firmness of *truth* eventually fades into dissipation of thoughts, leaving them equal to non-entities. So it is with truth everlasting; we must not hide our heads in shame for those thoughts we have forgotten. Just as simple as that, we forget many lessons.

It is always thus with mankind; he forgets the *truth,* the *laws* that were set down from the beginning for mankind to follow. We must condemn not ourselves, but rather condemn the period of forgetfulness that destroys or evades the issues of life. We have wanted to forget the *truth* in many instances. Life became easier to live if *truth* was forgotten. After subverting *truth* for long periods of time, we eventually were able to hide the *truth* from ourselves, for it was hidden deep within the chronicling of *truth* as was set down from the beginning of time. We evade the issues of *truth* by refusing to admit we know them. It is useless information, we tell ourselves, until finally we find trouble so great we cannot handle it. Then we mourn and wail at ourselves, thinking, "If only I could remember the *truth* as was set down by the Father from the beginning, I could solve all my problems."

Well, it wasn't meant to be. We were meant to forget our troubles so we could renew our lives again and again--renew our lives, start anew. Don't condemn yourself for forgetting the *truth* as was set down centuries ago. They still apply today, but consternation would result if we shouted from the rooftops: "We are slaves, we are not free men," as was our fate in a previous lifeline.

Who knows the real *truth* today? We are told man has long forgotten what he was taught in the beginning. Is it the animal or plant kingdom that knows best how to cope with life? The beast. For he seldom is in need of anything more than food for survival. Otherwise what disposition does he have to make for anything else but life here on earth?

The vegetable lives alone until life is uprooted and it is eaten. Yet it subsists for a long time until one or another, beast or man, crushes it. Yet it contributes its bit of energy to mankind and to the animal. It has fulfilled its life.

Downtrodden men escape their lives simply by mystical signs. They think. "If only the Holy One, blessed be His name, could find me, He would release me from this injustice that is being done unto me."

Who has the greater understanding of a lifetime here on earth? Dirt farmers understand their work; they understand the dirt, when to plant, when to fertilize, when to reap their crops. Yet, offer them another way of life and they are lost. So it is with mankind. Treat him to an earlier existence and he revolts, saying, "I don't belong here."

Thus the reason for the period of forgetfulness.

What we are trying to teach you is to remember that which is necessary to subsist in your daily life, but do not try to relive your past lifetimes. It wasn't meant to be.

Think these thoughts through. Eventually all of mankind will understand how to live according to the *laws* of the Lord. Ascend to heaven through the thought waves of *truth.*

CHAPTER 9

HERITAGE

We are crippling our souls with the heresy that God is only to be found in the dead roots of our present religions, as we now know them. We are cutting off our own birthright, our heritage as God's children.

God is *in* every phase of good that you do, every bit of beauty you see. All that is in nature is God's true personality. From the cleanness of mountain air to the freshness of morning dew on a lowly hollyhock. Go to nature's own bosom and see His wondrous hand. Everything He professed and taught was simplicity within itself.

It is when we start investing our beliefs with the trappings of insignificant grandeur that we lose the whole gist of a true religion. God meant us to inherit the true form of His way of life without its being diluted.

That is why we find ourselves in such confusion. We have been taught that religion is a living warmth that invades the body, soul, and heart, and thrills the mind. Only we find the manner in which it is presented today warps our thinking and freezes our hearts with its cold, majestic air. No, that is not what He wanted. He wanted us to come to Him dejected, sore of soul, and leave Him with a joy that would not confine itself to even ordinary expression. This is a moving force, this type of living. In the beginning when we lived close to the Father, we felt His embrace of love of life. He loved us all, and in return we adored Him. That is what He meant; that is how He wanted us to live--to live love. This: a heritage of courage, love, and humility.

We were born to this world merely to win our way back to our beloved Father. No one escapes it. There is but one road; that is His road. There is but one way; His way. Love all men and all will be made clear to you.

It is not easy, this living love, but through it lies salvation.

Man was not so constructed that he could exist without something bigger to sustain him. It was meant that we walk hand in hand with God. It should be so simple as to sit with Him and talk to Him as a trusted true friend. That is where we have missed the boat, so to speak. He was meant to be as much a part of our daily lives as the water we drink, the bread we eat. Faulty interpretations have given us a false impression of God.

Man generally learns faster through fear; therefore, early in the beginning of mankind, God was taught to people as a wrathful God, a vengeful monarch. Sure, it made man good, because he feared the consequences of his doing evil. God does not want His children to fear Him, to do what is right only because "all hellfire" will descend upon them. Herein lies the confusion. What

God taught was this: *If you surrender your life in My keeping, you can only live love, and, in so doing, can do no wrong. For love Me, because I am in every leaf, every shaft of sunlight. I am the air you breathe, the music you sing, the beauty you see, I am in everything. So despise not a single thing, for in so doing, you despise Me. I am in the heart of a stumbling sinner; I am in the blind endeavors of a self-righteous man, in the mistakes of a lonely woman. So despise Me not, for through God's light I will be made whole before your very eyes.*

No, waste not a single moment in judgment of another man, for he is working in the garments God has given him. They are not your garments, nor mine. Only God as the seamstress can mend a tear or put in stitches here and there. It is His work, not ours. So who is to say about the final garment? It is true a clean shift of homespun cloth is by far a finer raiment in the eyes of God than an ill-kept dirty piece of satin and lace. So remember God chose all materials as His own and the final decision is His, not ours.

All in life would be simple if we would but say each day, *"God, let my lips speak Your words; let my mind think Your thoughts; let my heart feel Your love. Then, my Lord can I say for this day I give thanks. I have lived it Your way."* All of the evil, all of the self-seeking could not exist.

We are due a rude awakening through fear; we will turn again inward to God. Often God uses our greed, our faulty judgment to bring us a new truth, as He is doing now. Wars are not of His making; as is in chaos, in most cases can we be brought to our knees. So if we but listen to His sweet soothing tones of, *"My children, My love, I send you in your great need, My love. Bring your heartfelt weariness to My well of everlasting peace that I might sponge your brow of discord and confusion. Rest and have done with the pettiness and the hates and deceits of a foolish paradise. I, your Lord, your God, wait and give homage to My long-suffering children. Turn to Me in your hour of need. I but wait to walk with you on the lonely paths. I give you all you need for your journey, only but surrender to Me."*

Would you not despise a father who would make his son go to endless petitions to but talk to his own "father"? Talk to God; make Him as easy to be with as the next door neighbor you love. Admit no formality. For there isn't a fear or a heartache you've had that He has not experienced with you. We needn't fear anything at all--name your greatest fear and it is nothing when it stands in the shadow of God's love. We need desperately in our time the sweet, soothing waves of God's love to flow over the earth, bathing all of His children in tolerance and love of each other.

God has said, "Love others as you love yourself," "Do unto others as you would have others do unto you."

One simple commandment. If we but lived by this one alone, we could inherit the kingdom of heaven.

How easy it is for us to give the best construction possible to all our endeavors, good or bad. Try doing it with your neighbor and a new world will open up to you. For the man you call enemy has the same heartaches, the same loneliness, and the same problems you have. Lend him your tools of love that he might repair his damages; lend him your shoulder that he might rest awhile; lend him your heart that he, too, might love anew. Do all this in God's name and you will build your own citadel, and in time find your way back home safely to the Father.

Life and Its Problems

We are all concerned with life and its problems. If someone were to tell you "In this store is an excelsior you can buy to solve all your difficulties," who could resist? The *truth* is so simple it has been overlooked, overrun, and ignored for the more intricate trappings of our lives today. It is far more sophisticated to say that I am finding peace of mind through my psychiatrist than finding peace of mind walking with God. We must get back to the simple way of flowing with God's good, His graces.

We have been taught, "Surrender to Me as little children." What is the most touching characteristic of children? Their faith and their love, without discrimination of any living thing. It's God's formula. He gave it to us once, and all we have to do is but listen and pray, and it's ours again--our heritage.

Without His anointment, all is lost. Money, fame, any other blessings you can think of are of no solace, not when the soul is in cold despair. We are a sorry people who have been led to believe that all that matters is the quest for material things; that it does not matter if a man sells his honor, love, self-respect--just as long as he climbs the ladder of success. Always the material.

We hear the hawkings of the blind of soul, of heart, saying: "You! All that matters in this world is you and your own selfish gains." "Get them or they will get you." "If you don't look out for yourself, who will?" These and many other expressions are but the quicksand of a life of despair, where we must forever be a slave to our own monster eyes.

The world is in no world-shaking danger of atomic destruction. Oh no, for years the eulogies of our times have done more to destroy our heritage of God than any such catastrophe. Our real danger lies in our own selfishness as a nation, and as individuals. What is so shocking to witness is the complete utter indifference of we humans to one another's needs. We are saying it matters not to me what happens to anyone, as long as it doesn't faze "Me, Inc." Even corporations who vie for the same customers realize that they must live by a form of exchange of good will. The company that tries to exist alone soon goes out of business. So it is with the individual.

God made us so that our very nature calls for the love of man for his family, his home, his fellow man. God meant us as little cells all living off the "Big Whole," which is God. So when we try to make it alone we wither and die inwardly. A soul sickens on self-love; it must bathe in the stream of love, the great love of its fellow man. He must live tolerantly, sending his best thoughts and actions to each man he meets. That is <u>all men,</u> not just a Baptist because he is a Baptist or a Catholic because he is a Catholic. No, it means all creeds, all colors, all religions. This is what God taught: by living together and loving each other, there is a workable solution to all living problems.

Through God, there is the control bar. Through

Him, there are no "off" days; all can be leveled off. We must condition ourselves to the belief that we are not bobbing like a cork on a turbulent sea. Rather, we are a sturdy craft with a good skipper at the controls.

We must learn to surrender to God. In the morning, awaken by saying, *"May God bless the efforts of this day. I surrender myself in Your keeping, Father. Bless my decisions; lead me to my highest good. Bend me; make me into the pattern You have made for me."* Ask God to lift you up to His level, never pray to have Him come down to you. In that way, you become the masterpiece. All is possible through God, who gives you strength and love.

How to Inherit Our Legacy

Now in our present time it is far harder to inherit our legacy of God's love. We have too great a respect for the material and not near enough regard for the spiritual. We have inherited the blunders of a people bent on a scientific explanation of all things. "It must weigh one pound or be thirty-six inches to the yard." With these tools of knowledge we must give solace to a soul that can only grow on the intangible. It must be fed with good work, tolerance and love of his fellow man-- which on the scales of worth weighs exactly nothing.

So we must harken back and learn to hew out the laws of a comforting religion, a way of life that can withstand all misconceptions and pathetic ignorance. We have been promised a "Living Font," only to learn we have inherited a passion stream. This is not God's way; this is not what He intended for His beloved children. Through the ages it has been changed, this word of God, by a fearful people, until little is left of the original *truth*. Little minds and great fears have made this true religion into a pattern of intolerance and arrogance. The religions we now know have withstood the ravages of time, but not the ravages of souls stumbling in darkness and fear. Men found that it was easier to teach others to respect a wrathful monster than to love a bountiful master.

They had no faith in love, only in suppression, in seeking to band together in closed groups to perpetuate their conception of religion. If men would have opened their eyes and hearts, the hungers of their souls could have been satisfied.

So we find ourselves in this century merely victims of a fear-guided people, mistreating one another, setting ourselves against each other. We are <u>all</u> God's children. All, He embraces us all--all religions, all colors, all nations, and once we realize that He is working in all of us, trying to rise to the surface, we will then open the door of love and let Him in to bathe us in the goodness of <u>His</u> way of life. He wants but to walk with us, lead us home. So take Him in as a beloved friend and let Him forever cast a shadow over your paths.

"Oh God, give me the grace and the foresight to learn by this experience." When we realize that we are not objects of a cruel, vengeful God we will learn to accept each trial, each tribulation as a hurdle that we must overcome as part of our Olympics of survival. Ask God for the lesson we must learn so that we might profit and go on. For each heartache, each problem is but the part we must play in life's drama. As brick by brick we build our temple, so it is with our building of character in God's holy image. No one is sent a finished product; each and everyone is sent his own salvation. No two are alike: each is equipped by a wise Father with the tools he will need so that he may build his life and finish the roadway back home safely to the Father.

Live One Day At a Time

When once we learn to become master of all we

contact, we have then tapped in on the supreme way of life. Just think of the tremendous scope of complete mastery over self. We could then live without the chains of self-doubt, of inner defeat, and turn our efforts to the building of the truly important truths. There would be little to deprive us of our heritage.

It is not easy, this mastery of self. In fact, once embarking on this feat of seeking within to change, to build and to master, we will find an overwhelming amount of defeatism. We must change every bad fault for a good one, and although we men are transgressors back for soul growth, each time--if we are keeping alert-- we will learn and grow until man himself is a miracle of God's love as he was intended to be.

Worry not about the body's appetites; all can be brought under the law of moderation. All can become servants of the soul as was intended. Man's worth in this world is his exchange on the spiritual market, not on the material market. That is where the final reckoning will be, and that is the phase of living we must concern ourselves with above all others.

If we are vigilant in the effort of spiritual growth, the rest will flow with us. We need not concern ourselves completely with the survival of the material; God has promised He will provide our daily needs. He did not tell us He would provide weeks in advance. We must live but one day at a time. So pray, *"Please, Father, I do not pray for tomorrow, but this is what I need today. Please provide for me today."*

You see, my dear ones, if we can make one day at a time our complete victory, we then have the beginning of a successful life. We were so created that we must face and live hour by hour, day by day.

If we forget the weight of the yesterdays and the fears of the tomorrows, we are halfway through our mastery over the life that we are now living and that we came to live in order to finish that which we did not do at another time.

Clean Out Your Closets

In any endeavor we undertake, we find it best to "clear the desk," so to speak, of any unfinished business before we start another task. Each night we should rid the soul of any failure or misgiving we have taken on that day. Undress the heart and soul each night so in the morning you can start anew. It is a very wise idea to get rid of any driftwood of the past that we are unconsciously carrying with us.

Sit down; write the things that you have done that bog you down with unhappiness. See if there is any restitution that you might do to repay the wrong or debt. So often it will be a simple "I'm very sorry; forgive me" that will heal an open wound. Perhaps it is a debt unpaid. Pay it. Clean out your closets, dust out the corners, let in God's light. When we are not chastising ourselves for an ill-spent yesterday, we can live victoriously in the present day. All of us are carrying around barnacles of guilt that weigh us down. Make a clean sweep of it all.

Once and for all, make a new start. It can be done only by taking away the feeling of guilt which we all carry.

Do three things:

1. Find out why you feel <u>responsible</u> for this debt.

2. Make <u>restitution</u> to the best of your ability.

3. Close the door on it and <u>forget</u> it.

If you do this, you can start a life of rebirth without the weight of guilt. You can travel God's road with a lighter step.

God meant us to live like this. Forget the yesterdays; live this present day with anticipation and acceptance of God's good. We must only face one second at a time. He made certain laws that govern all lives. He was a wise creator. He knew that we must be equipped to live minute by minute. If a giant generator would start missing its tempo, the engineer would immediately know he was in for grave trouble. So it is with us. We are living a tempo that makes for easier living.

So stop fretting and fearing, and exist in God's love.

Roadmap For Truth

Living--just existing--has its own problems. When we add the guilty feelings and frustrations that beset us, we have a constant state of confusion. In this article we are going to try to give you a roadmap for living in truth. It doesn't mean that you can't embrace your present religion. This is just the guidebook to help you in your present beliefs.

We know that we must lessen our load of worldly cares. God specified this on many occasions. Once we start to strip ourselves down to <u>true essentials</u>, we will start accomplishing our desires.

Concentrate on prayer and ask God's help in all you do; then just relax and let Him take over. All will be so much easier when you never feel alone, when you feel the shadow of a loving presence in all you do.

We all realize that living is not child's play. We don't promise that if you follow this advice life will be a rose-strewn path, but we do say that life can be met with anticipation and courage.

Thus we give you the weapon to make life less threatening to man. When men are sent into battle, they are not assured victory. But they are given weapons and fighting techniques to make it possible. It is true most of us want to put out as little effort as possible and discover some morning that a miracle has taken place in our lives, in our world. That isn't God's way. He sends us the faith, the tools, but lets <u>us</u> do our own building.

No one ever appreciated the easier things that were acquired with little effort. Our Father knew when He made men as complex as He did that in man's seeking, he'd find the well-marked road; that after wandering aimlessly in a wilderness, a path to God would be most welcome.

Guideposts to Happier Living

We all must have guideposts to live by. We try the hodge-podge system and become hopelessly lost. The heart was meant to feel its own happy tempo in life with God.

We have winter, the happy awakening of spring, and the full realization of summer. This is nature's cycle. So it is with us. We follow our cycles, too. We were meant to get lost, to seek then the lighthouse of God's living. We must seek and find all our lives. This is one of our guideposts to happier living: realizing that when we are temporarily lost, it is not because God has shut His door on us. No, He knows that He must constantly refresh us in His waters. If we were not famished for His waters, could we fully realize their therapy? He, in His goodness, gave us contrasts in that we have a good-bad, love-hate, loyalty-disloyalty. If it all flows to us in abundance, would we look inward? Look at some of your most fortunate of people--fortunate, that is, in the material of this world. They are existing in a so-called Shangri-La. Are they happy, or do they resemble squirrels in a cage?

So obviously our Maker knew what He was about when He planted a seed of soul growth within us. So be not dismayed when momentarily we are blinded by our own shortcomings. Just turn inward; the answer lies there. Ask God to let you follow His path. Soon you'll be trodding on God's path again, guideposts clearly pointing the way.

This you must remember: there isn't a human being walking the earth, humble or great, who isn't following this pattern. So have faith; you are not alone in your dark moments. Every man who has passed your way has carried the same problems and has had to seek his own salvation.

There are too many real dangers we must face to waste our energy on fighting ourselves. "Know thyself" is a wise proverb. Yes, learn to know the inner working of yourself. Get at peace with the soul. It is not easy, this task, for we hold on very desperately to our weaker selves.

It is hard to throw off a bad habit and give birth to a positive new one. God knew of this; that is why He gave us soul growth--to sustain us in all of our "re-embarking." Once you learn to live without the crutches of self-excusing, you will be well on the way to successful living.

How many of us find ourselves believing that all we construct is perfect? Next time we see this trait in ourselves, we should check it and examine it in the critical eye of our worst critic. Then we will start a balance in ourselves. Be as kind to others in your judgment as you would want them to be with you. On the other hand, turn the fault finding inward. It is the perfect answer to mastery over self.

Self-mastery is one of the hardest of taskmasters, but there isn't a successful man alive who didn't first have to whip "the inner man" into shape.

We, in this day, are very conscious of the irritations of everyday living. The delays, the endless putting up with what we term the stupidity of "others," the increased tempo of our living, the pressure produced by a world bent on glorifying the material, leave men exhausted and spent. Man may well inquire, "How can I remain serene and calm in the face of all this?" True, it is not easy. God didn't promise us an easy path to paradise. He told us it would be filled with rocks, thistles, and thorns. He also gave us an inner power to help us over the obstacles, to rub balm on our lacerations.

He gave us a faith, an undying zeal for good. He gave us all we need to sustain us. He doesn't tell us to knock and He'll let us in; He would say, "Open the door and let <u>yourself</u> in. I am waiting for you."

CHAPTER 10

ACCEPTANCE

Acceptance - Surrender

We must have some partnership to sustain us to live and to survive in a world filled with confusion and danger. 'With whom?" you may ask yourselves. Often we give of ourselves to find that where we plant our seeds of love grow only weeds of despair. God knew of this and He knew that few of us attain greatness or goodness, that we are filled with human weaknesses, that we are bound to fail one another. That is why He stressed surrender all your heartache unto Him, so you can live. He knew we could not cope with all of the human weaknesses alone. He knew mankind needed an anchor that he might steady his craft and keep it from drifting into stormy seas, keeping it off dangerous reefs. So He often reminded us that our answer was to have faith and depend on Him and only Him; that the storms of man's folly could not swamp us. He realizes that in man himself as a human being, little was concrete; that we are all liquid beings taking on the shape of whatever receptacle we are filling at that moment. He bade us find in Him the never-changing security of His great love. He made us this way so we were incomplete, filled with a restlessness that gives us little peace so we will strive to reach higher and try harder to find our way back. We were not given a soul as a heritage; we were only lent one, and if we fail to keep up our payments on this loan we lose it again. He meant it to be so, for in this world of the material, if it gave complete satisfaction, we would soon lose the reason for our being here.

We all need a formula for successful living. None of us, none was sent it as a birthright. Surely you now understand how hard it is to reweave that tapestry that you left unwoven and will awaken to the responsibility you have in this lifetime.

"Seek and ye shall find." All have destiny; all have purpose. It rests with you to fulfill your destiny.

Do Not Accuse Man of Negativity

"Judge not lest ye be judged." Accept the goodness of mankind. If you look for negativity within a person, it will only bring forth an attempt by that person to defend this weakness by denial and cover-up. Sending thoughts of love and understanding can lend support and allow the individual to come to understand his shortcomings and so permit him to judge himself. Many times his heartache is more than he alone can bear. He finds it necessary to tell someone of his troubles. Giving of your time to listen to his burdens helps him to unload the anguish of his heart and may, in turn, save his life.

The accused man stands ready to defend himself; thus, no solution can be obtained in any way. We are not sent as judges, so we should accept man's faults. We have no right to accuse man of intent to be negative. He must recognize his own weaknesses and rid himself of his self-hatred which festers within himself. His own heartache is accusation enough. Mankind has a difficult enough time just living. Why should mankind multiply this inner disharmony by accusing another of wrongdoing? It creates a real injustice. If you must accuse someone of negativity, allow it to be yourself, as you are permitted to be your own judge.

It is important to dwell upon the positive aspects of someone's character, thus lending support for him to take action to fulfill his destiny in life. His intent, his purpose in life, extends into the unknown. Who among us knows another's purpose or destiny? How then can one stand in judgment of another? No man can change the future that has been preordained for him. His destiny rides in the balance, as whether he fulfills it or not depends upon him alone.

How To Think When Things Disturb You

We must learn to listen. If you listen quietly, you will hear the still, small voice from within. Hear and listen for evidences of truth around you. First, learn how to relax. Start by heaving a huge sigh of relief; then, inflate your lungs. Take at least six deep breaths, think pure thoughts: How high is that mountain? How blue is the sky? How clean is the air?

Allow yourself to think these pleasant thoughts of universal surroundings; how beautiful the mountains are, and how harmonious the song of the bird. Thus you become more harmonious with your surroundings. "How could I have let anything disturb me? Why don't I listen to the universal law of peace and harmony instead of this disturbing thought?"

Now you must let go. Imagine yourself floating on a

fleecy white cloud. Imagine you are lying in a hayloft. At this time you cease to exist among the negative thoughts that are disturbing you. It is when you say, *"I exist in spirit now; I am allowing my spirit--my soul--to soar. Now I shall listen to the still, small voice within --that of my higher self I shall feel and sense great love. I shall not allow myself to harbor any resentment against any person or for any cause to disturb me whatsoever."* If you feel resentment for any person, say, *"I don't want ill health or any harm to come to this person. I want only this person's happiness. May God bless this individual."*

Then say to yourself, *"I observe these Laws of Truth. I am rewarded by the Masters of Truth. Now I shall observe these thoughts whenever I am displeased by any negative thought. I shall wipe it out of my mind by observing the universe and its laws."*

"I shall allow myself to see the stars bright at night. I shall observe and respect the heavens above me

studded with stars that illuminate the way safely back home to the Father."

"I shall observe His laws. My destiny depends upon my observing these laws. I will sense a new beginning for the universe as well as for myself as I observe the laws, as I progress on my way down the pathway of life."

In observing these truths. I set into motion a life worth living without fear. The Father leads us straight forward into eternity. Our faith and trust in Him never waivers.

Freedom of thought eliminates all negativity. If we say we are free men, we are free by declaring we are free. We are observing the *Laws* the Father sent to us. These *Laws* help us avoid the holocausts that may occur. If we establish the kingdom of heaven on this planet upon which we live, then we continue to live. The law we establish is the kingdom of heaven for all of mankind.

For instance, if I salute the flag each time I see it, won't it inspire others to salute the flag? Similarly, will we not establish the kingdom of heaven here upon the earth plane by establishing the kingdom of heaven within our own minds?

There is no end to these ideas of how to establish a kingdom of heaven within our minds or how to think when things disturb us. We have to learn how to escape to a haven of refuge within our minds.

Harbor no ill will against any man. Allow everyone his freedom of thought; permit him to act as he will.

You must learn to ignore insults or lies, or injuries. You must refuse to think about them or to speak of them. Some men are depraved. Even though it might not seem so today--what about tomorrow? Will the culprit be filled with remorse or truth? Who is to judge? Set all discord aside and bless them. Place them and the discordant incidents into the hands of the Father. In so doing, you follow your own directions and you cannot be harmed.

We Have Forgotten How to Pray

We have forgotten how to pray to the Father. We beseech Him only when we are in trouble or during troubled times; never only just to seek his comfort, or just to tell Him we love Him and to thank Him for all the blessings He has heaped upon us.

We think we have no negative ways, and so we devote our lives to living along without His help and guidance. It is most important that we ask daily for His guidance and direction.

"Thy will be done, Oh Father, Thy will."

Each time you pray and feel close to the Father, your Master, ask for divine guidance and seek it truthfully. *"I am here, Father. Gathered together tonight with Your children, lead us out of the wilderness and darkness to our destiny, to the light. Lead us out of trouble to the greener pastures promised to us. Guide and direct our lives, Oh Father, for You are the one and only God over all mankind."*

Indeed, the Sermon on the Mount was meant for humble man to think of God first. For if we believe in the Father always, first above ourselves, He will respond. He avoids us if we distrust Him, but if as little children we trust Him as we hope our children trust in us as parents, then He obliges us with His answers to our prayers and thoughts.

Do not turn the other cheek; rather, turn your face upward to the Father. Use the Lord's light wisely. The greatest asset you have is your light, your imagination. Use it diligently and intelligently. Educate yourself not to weaken under pressure of people's doing harm to you. God equates weakness with negativity.

If someone hurts you, turn your face upward and

say, *"Here I am, Father. I object to being treated in this manner."* You then establish a precedent. If you are truly hurt, He joins with you in helping you find the answer to ease that hurt. Once you establish this precedent of using the "upturned face," no one can truly hurt you, for you will immediately say. *"Father, teach me to dispel this hurt from my mind."*

Negativity destroys the useful part of mankind's mind. If you choose this manner of "upturned face" thinking, it will ease the troubles of your mind. You are using the Father's healing light. Try always to use His healing power for solace, never for revenge. Use the Lord's healing light wisely.

Acceptance- 144

CHAPTER 11

FORGIVENESS

Burdens of Life

The Father lives close to each of us, within us. Do not allow anyone to erase that thought from your mind. Do not accept any teaching that says the Father does not exist. The truth is that He is very much alive and is within each and every man.

Mankind hovers around with all his burdens in view, hoping that the Father will see these burdens and give him freedom from them; but in truth, what would be learned if the burdens fell from his shoulders and he did not have to strain any more? He would indeed learn nothing. The Father observes the burdens and guides us past all obstacles that might trip us and cause us to fall. He helps clear the way for our reunion; He clears the way for us to be reunited with our peers. Sad is the day and sad is the night when we are separated from our peers, because we are suited to be with one another. We think alike, yet we chose to be separated this time on earth to learn our lessons. Yet actually part of us waits for that reunited state to be able to share that which we have learned during this period of separation. It is sad to know that there are peers around us that we do not recognize as beings who have so often softened our load or burden in other lifetimes.

It saddens us to see father and child hate each other, destroy the bond of affection that flies out the window through a disagreement or misunderstanding. Yet it happens all the time. Still, when they are reunited again, the bond is even greater. So abide in the Father and dispel the thought that the Father lives in a singular solitary person. He lives in <u>us all</u>. It is sad to think how our lives might be without Him around us, surrounding us with His love and understanding. What we don't understand while we're carrying all these heavy burdens alone is that solace awaits us, if only we knew how to reach out to solicit His aid.

Needless burdens outweigh our belief in the Lord. Solitary feelings of loneliness, sadness caused by disbelieving our fellow human beings whom we trusted. Those who violated our confidence--they all feel sad, too. They know the truth, and yet somehow they refuse to revise their lives. They live in fear of being found out by having the shirt or cloak of decency ripped from their shoulders. We must bless them and set them free, and again search for those friends that we can love and trust.

It is sad, but true, in this lifetime that so much of this distrust exists. Man against man--nation against nation. But those who follow the words of the Lord seldom distrust others. If deserted or misused, they continue to follow the Lord's words of forgiveness.

Reincarnation

For the Western world, belief in reincarnation is new. To the Eastern world, the idea of reincarnation is as old as the rising and setting of the sun. Each of us has a certain identity--or signal, if you will. The possibility of this identity persists through a long series of lifetimes. It casts off worn-out bodies and personalities, perhaps as a snake sheds its outer skin. The ultimate destination is perfection, enlightenment, and joy. There was never a time when we did not exist, nor will there be any future time we shall cease to be. Bodies may die, but the soul which inhabits the body is eternal.

The permanent identity of self, the soul, transcends and outlives the transient personality of each successive incarnation. The task of every soul is to recognize itself, to be itself, yet to be one with the creative lifeforce: God. Even when we finally achieve perfection or oneness with God, we also maintain our individuality or our signal to the very end of time. We have our own uniqueness.

Whether we believe in eternal identity or not, one undeniable, inescapable fact pertains to us all: the fact of human suffering. How are we to escape? How are we to free ourselves of the frustrations and agonies that torment human lives? Finally, how are we to live in freedom and joy? Which is the way?

Essentially, life is a spiritual force and must be interpreted as a continuous experience. Ignorance of karma and reincarnation may be a hindrance to spiritual progress. The continuous experience would hardly benefit us without our understanding first karma, then reincarnation.

Certainly beautiful and fruitful lives have lived without its knowledge. Countless men and women of many religious faiths have lived saintly lives without any knowledge of, or belief in reincarnation. However, at a certain stage of evolution, a knowledge of reincarnation is indispensable for full comprehension of one's self and of life eternal.

The final redemption of self can be understood without consciously dredging up the past, and by consciously casting off the negativity so dredged up.

Often I am asked how one learns about one's past:

1. Relive it through hypnosis and memory.

2. Have a mystic relate the story.

3. By meditation and analysis of one's dreams.

It is not enough to know that one wore a monk's habit, or was a king, or a riverboat pilot. The psychology of the personality is most important, for that delineates the significant traits of that life, and that personality created the complications of the present life.

We all fantasize, but there must also be a psychological, valid relationship in terms of moral cause and effect between the past lives and the present.

We then seek knowledge to help us obey the laws we already know and use what we do know, *The Laws* that bring us closer to perfection. We are back then to the divine triangle.

1. To liberate ourselves from this world, we must gather strength and the three divine attributes with which we were endowed from the beginning of time.

2. We must seek out and learn the laws of life and death.

3. We must acquire knowledge and pursue science; ignorance is surely unworthy of man who was created by God.

We must try to bring ourselves into intelligent harmony with the laws we have discovered; with our souls, we must try to seek love. By loving, we find happiness within ourselves. By loving, we begin work with dedication in the world as we were meant to do-- dedicated for the sake of making life beautiful for all, and not for the sake of personal reward.

If we keep uppermost the thought of God instead of our own ego, we will surely lose the illusionary ego attachments that fasten us to the wheel of misery and the endless rounds of birth and death. Love is ever the greatest force within us.

St. Francis was hoeing in his garden and was asked what he would do if the world should end that night. After he thought for a moment, he replied, "I would continue to hoe my garden."

Today we are faced with the most terrible threat of planetary destruction, global war, total annihilation. What a sense of futility, of waste, of horror!

But all this need not occur.

Everything that happens, all our experiences, are opportunities, the materials from which we weave the tapestry of our lives and from which we win salvation.

This is our garden. We must set about our Father's business by hoeing that garden.

CHAPTER 12

REINCARNATION

Four Emotions

Many men doubt the existence of afterlife. As we have noted before, reincarnation is not generally accepted by Western man. But those of you who do believe there is a life after so-called death (we say "so-called" for those of us who believe in reincarnation) know that we simply pass from one state of existence to another--from carnal to spiritual.

When the spirit first realizes that he has, indeed, been separated from his physical body, he experiences four emotions. They are not experienced one after the other immediately. But like the child learning first to crawl, how to stand, and then to walk, so it is in our spiritual growth. After we leave our physical bodies, the first emotion is *fear*--fear of the unknown. The second emotion is _helplessness_, for we know not how to take that first step forward--just as it took us time to take our first step in our physical body. The third emotion is _loneliness,_ for we have to learn how to communicate just as we had to learn how to speak. The fourth emotion brings great elation, for it is _discovery_!

CHAPTER 13

PARABLES

Putting Your House in Order

Once there lived a pontiff who was rich in land and wisdom. He had two beautiful daughters who were rich in nothing but this world's goods. Now it came to pass that although people came from far and near to hear his great wisdom, he was an absolute deaf-mute to those near and dear to him.

One daughter, the elder, was cruel and heartless. Her serpent tongue always found its mark. She was loved by few. The younger was a consort for all men. No man of low birth or high could call her stranger. All this the great one knew, and it weighed heavily on his shoulders. He knew not what to do. He was wont to say, "Why is it I, who am so full of wisdom, who is so good, who is without sin, was sent a spheme such as these two? I don't deserve it. It is I who have been put upon by the Lord."

Years went by. He was cursed with his unwanted daughters, although they were beautiful and wealthy. No one would marry the shrew with the wicked tongue, nor could he find a mate for his much "mated" younger daughter. So he accepted all this with great curses and continued on his lonely way, expounding great wisdom and accumulating still more wealth.

Now it came to pass that he was confined to his chambers because of great swelling of his old joints. For the first time in many years, he was aware of the house around him. In his despair, he saw his daughters as his personal curses. While he was lying abed, his daughter's faithful maid servant--she who had suckled the younger and elder along with her own--was afoot. He looked at her unlined face heavy with her inner peace, her thick, busy body. He knew this one was four score and twenty.

Why was she so blessed? Wasn't he the anointed one? This he asked her: "Why your amenable disposition? Where are your plagues? Have you not ungrateful children such as I?"

"No, old wise one," answered his faithful servant. "When you were busy making a great name as a mansion of wisdom, I was putting my house in order. I listened to my young. I gathered them about my knee. I gave them the wisdom of God's great love. When they stumbled, I picked them up, ever telling them of the beauty of walking upright. Soon they were as sure-footed as little goats. When it was time for them to meet the world, they were seasoned in all things and made strong by love."

At this point the old monarch said, "But what could you give your children that I could not? I have wealth, power, great wisdom. People from hundreds of leagues away come to hear me speak so eloquently. You mean that you have more wisdom than I, ungracious one?"

"No," answered the servant, "just more heart have I. Yes, I have seen your daughters falter. Didn't I suckle them with my own child when their mother took leave of this house? Didn't the elder always respond to a kind word when she was young, before the great frost of your criticism bit into her soul? You taught her not only to hate and despise, but to flog with her tongue because she is lost in the fog of your great injustice. The younger--didn't she always need love as the earth needs rain? Now she takes her moisture from any pool, muddy or clear. What care she? It is your starvation and turning your waters of love and understanding to another land, and letting your own lands lay parched and plagued with disease. This I will say unto you, great lord. Get in order your own dwelling. Make it first the temple; then make the world a better place to live in!"

The Sparrow and the Missionary

Now on top of a high mountain lived a missionary who thought he knew all the answers as to why he was living. He thought he could answer all the questions: What am I doing here? Why am I living alone high on the mountaintop?

Once a sparrow landed on top of the mission roof, feeling that he would be safe in this particular sanctuary. He sat there for a moment, wondering if he could communicate with the missionary. Soon the missionary sat down upon the ground. Looking up to the sparrow, he began to speak. He started his conversation by saying, "Can you tell me why you are living?" The sparrow sat there for a moment, dumbfounded to think that a minister would use so crude a beginning.

"How do you know I have a purpose on earth?"

The missionary answered, "Why, we all have, don't

we?"

Now the sparrow thought for a moment, then replied, "Yes, we all have a mission on earth. What is yours, pray tell?"

The missionary sat still for a moment contemplating the answer. Then the sparrow spoke up, asking, "How long has it been since you guided a family so that they might feel secure within their lives, so that they might know how to find the pathway home to the Father, so that they might know how to be self-sufficient? How long has it been since you actually thought about the Father and the direction your life has taken?"

Then the sparrow spoke again, saying, "I know my mission here on earth. I follow the directions I am given. I follow my instincts. I follow the divine law. I rid your land of beetles and pests that destroy your crops. I maintain an equilibrium of nature so that your foodstuffs will grow and your land will not be overrun with insects and grasshoppers, and thus I retain control of my destiny."

The sparrow continued, "How far have you come along this line of thinking? Have you guarded the secrets the Lord sent back with you? Do you fully understand the message I have brought here to you? Do you understand that each man, woman, child, beetle-- yes, even the lowly beetle--has a duty to perform so that the united front or equilibrium of mankind can exist and be maintained?"

As he spoke, he took wing and left the sanctuary and the security provided him by the mission. He went seeking higher ground and more understanding. Thus we learn an object lesson. The missionary was dumb, but thought he was smart in questioning the lowly sparrow about his truth; while, all along, he himself was unsure of his own worth.

<u>Thinking Independently</u>

Once, high on the mountain, we found ourselves alone with the Father. He had secluded Himself from mankind and left us alone to see what thoughts we could discover for ourselves. He allowed us to talk to one another, communicate as we communicate today. A pall of silence fell upon our group, for we had run out of subject matter. The doctor among us exclaimed, "Hear no evil, see no evil, feel no evil."

The others said similar things, but soon we had run out of ideas. Then the Lord gazed down upon us, saying, "Hear no evil, say no evil, but look around yourself for evil and then avoid it by sidestepping it."

He counseled with us, then said, "Look around you. We have manufactured a machine to help you think thoughts unknown today."

We allowed the machine to direct our thinking. We thought whatever the machine directed us to think. At last we began to lose the ability to think independently, on our own.

The Lord looked down His nose at us again and said, "How do you like the thinking machine?"

We all exclaimed in one breath, "It is wonderful that we do not have to think for ourselves; but on the other hand, we dislike being told what, how, and how soon to think. We prefer our own independent thoughts."

He held us close to His heart and said, "Hallelujah, you have awakened to the *truth* today. You have finished your own thoughts. It is important to think independently and to look ahead into the future by yourself."

For the Lord manifests the *truth* individually for each of us to learn alone. Only those thought waves that you seek can be found within your mind. Look into the future and fear not. The Lord is beside you.

How He Taught Us to Live

First He chose a few masters to learn the *truth*. Yes, then He told them, "You go into the wilderness which is what you know as the world, and teach these thoughts unto others."

He immediately declared that thoughts are sacred, and the masters somehow knew that this was a *Universal Truth*. The masters dispensed it among the slaves as well as all others who would listen to them. But soon He called to the masters with additional directions. He said, "Go out into the wilderness and seek higher learning. There is much to expose yourself to. Seek the higher thought waves that float loosely around the earth; seek the higher teachings, not the lower. If you accept the lower teachings we cannot instill further thoughts into your mind."

So the masters gathered their belongings and went seeking truth. Soon they came to a large river, and there stood a man. He instructed them how to cross the river, and he told them how to seek the higher road: "Yes, the lower land will flood further up the way," he said, "and you will drown. If you do not come into sight soon, I shall come looking for you."

The Lord stood there dressed as a man, and the masters in their search for higher ground had found the Father.

Then there was the crossroad which they came upon, and further down the road they saw a haven waiting for them and a guide to direct them. He taught them these things singularly, and worked with them until they learned how to harvest the green foodstuffs. From His back He carried them into the high countries and taught them all the amenable thoughts unknown in your land today.

He started with the first thought: *"Calm your heart and soul and accept the light I send thee; accept the life on earth as a proving ground, an exertion on your part to solve your problems with the help of those who choose to surround you. Solve the problems you have both with us and those with whom you live."*

The Father anoints us with oil on our heads when we seek a reprieve from our fate, but He insists we continue to think deeply and seek the higher land, the higher learning. The land, the earth upon which you stand, is imaginary; it is all a dream or illusion of thought.

The Lesson of the Lost Lamb

On a large mountainside, many men and women were gathered together within a circle. Each was counting off his herd of sheep. After this was finished, each took off alone in different directions. There was one sheepherder who was having difficulty getting his herd to leave the mountain pass. He did not realize that one of the mother sheep had discovered she had lost her baby.

She stampeded the herd and would not allow them to move. "Wait," she cried, "until I regain possession of my baby. Then we shall proceed down the mountain."

When the herdsman learned of her difficulty, he started searching the area for the lost lamb. He found her baby alive. It had fallen into a crevice and was covered over by high weeds. As soon as the joyous mother learned that her baby was safe, she signaled the herd to leave and they joyously went off to the lowlands, following the sheepherder.

Unlike human beings who abandon their babies, the mother waited for the herder to learn of her loss by showing him that she was searching. He, in turn, helped her find the baby and actually recovered it from the shallow grave into which it had fallen.

The Lord is such a Father. He always watches over His herd, and His losses are few. We may walk away and leave Him, but never does He lose sight of us. Each night He gathers his "kids" together as did the lamb's mother, and helps to harness their energy in such a fashion as to stampede the herd on the road to righteousness.

CHAPTER 14

PREPARING FOR ETERNAL LIFE

The Natural Phenomenon of Preparing for Death

Syndrome: A group of signs and symptoms that occur together and characterize a particular abnormality.

The syndrome 'til death do us part leads mankind to a pathway of destruction. We fear death and want to survive forever, whatever the cost may be. Rather, we should learn to accept our reward by looking forward to the next part of our life which takes us into a higher state of being or evolvement. In other words, look forward to a reward in heaven with the Father.

Even though that thought has been taught over the centuries, men still fear death more than any other phenomenon they have to face. Do people speak of death openly? No. Man is afraid he will be doomed to death just as many people fear that once they have a Will prepared, they will die.

When someone dies, what does mankind do but mourn for him. Rather, they should glorify his name and be happy for the peaceful solution that has come about for him.

We should understand that each man has to walk this pathway and that it will ultimately lead us to the next phase of living. Until man understands how important a part the end of life plays in Life Everlasting, mankind will continue to walk through the darkness of ignorance.

When we are deceased, it is the first time mankind seems to awaken to the fact that death is inevitable for all of us. During the years of our lifetime on earth, we march to a certain drummer all our own. We refuse to face the inevitable as we continue to walk aimlessly on the pathway of our lives without giving any forethought to the time we must return to another state of living. When the time comes and when the Maker wills us back, we seldom see a dry eye among our family or friends. To the contrary, we should never mourn or cry. We should rejoice and say, "Amen," for the Lord's will has been manifested through death. Our loved one's energy is reunited with the Maker once again.

Because of man's misconceptions and fears, he does not allow himself to think about death. Since it is inevitable, should you not plan ahead of time for your return to the Father?

How is this done? Meditators and those seeking to live in the light can simply discuss this with their Masters and Teachers and with the Maker Himself during periods of meditation. They should ask to be taught the ABCs, the basics, to help discipline the mind to allow them to emerge into the golden light of their existence.

What does man do? He wants to wander aimlessly, endlessly, looking for the golden light alone rather than trying to become acquainted with his Masters and Teachers for that takes a lot of dedication, effort and structure. He does not realize that when he meditates, his Masters and Teachers instruct him concerning his own signal or the exact phrases that he must learn in order to facilitate and make simpler the transition to the next phase of being.

It is often said that when the student is ready, the teacher appears. When that time comes in your life when you have evolved to the level of intelligence where you are in contact with your Masters and Teachers, they will teach you what you have to know.

It is also said that when man is born, the exact date of his return is also noted. The Masters record the date when one will be deceased; they wait then to handle all of the details to welcome him back. They try to put him at ease and remove any fears that he has brought with him. In this manner it makes the transition a more simple one.

Thus they will say unto the newcomer, "Welcome home. The challenge of the past lifetime is over."

Reactivating The Mind

The Father taught us *Truth* by eliminating the negative force that lives within mankind's mind. When man's mind is quiet and active, it allows us to teach him *truths*. Your mind, as an example, is alive and active today and welcomes us at different times; varying levels of your energy affect our efforts. If only mankind would let us take them forward into the kingdom of heaven and teach them to finish with every part of their past, man's life could be happy, healthy, and in a state of euphoria. By this I mean, if man could finish and repair the tapestry of his life—finishing those things carried over from the past—mankind could live the happy existence that he dreams about here and now.

Indifference among man seems to cause a sullying of his energy light, so to speak. He should allow his mind to go forward unto the end of time by driving all negativity from his mind. As we have frequently taught you, mankind lives on forever; there is no end to time. Energy is accumulated each time we live from the good deeds and honorable lives we lead and that energy is deposited on earth. We have referred to this as having an exchange of energy with your fellowman. Then when we return to live on the earthplane again, we forget how to regulate that energy; we forget how to work out our own differences from past lifetimes. We forget how to use our minds or think in order to be able to tap into the energy we left from our last lifetime on earth or the original source of energy that we have left behind on the other side.

All Things Spring from God

Teach men to <u>seethe not</u>, to <u>live not in anger</u>, for it costs him dearly of his earned energy. How to tap into the original energy source is somehow at first hidden from our sight, but what we have to do is to relearn where the source remains hidden. In other words, we have to learn how to listen to the wind and to the songs of the birds and to learn to live close with God's nature. This brings peace and harmony within, thus not using up energy as one does in anger. Understand that all are of His creation. Learning and living this will help activate our minds. So much is lost when we seethe with anger. Even we over here are truly soothed when man becomes more calm and complacent. This unfortunately does not usually occur among mankind until they reach the more mature or elderly state. Try to help your peers at all age levels to seek the higher frame of mind and thinking. You must learn to adjudicate the responsibility of living peacefully to all of mankind. Just do your best to guide and direct your fellowmen to the highest level of thinking. After helping them as much as you can in this way, it then becomes their responsibility. You say to them, "You must remember you have to learn how to think for yourself and bring peace to your consciousness, for each man commences to die the moment he is born."

Since we all know that we begin to die upon rebirth, why are we so afraid of dying? Ask yourself this question honestly and answer truthfully. The truthful answer should be that we only have to hope that we have finished our destiny or mission before we expire. Therefore, with the completion of our destiny, there should be no fear of the dying experience. All men are afraid of the unknown and all men dislike change—thus death becomes a fearful part of life for them, even though each man knows that death is inevitable.

It is disturbing to us on this side that those of you who are living and evolving upon the earth refuse to listen to *Truth*. It is almost that you say, "Leave me alone." But mankind must strive to understand that if he really wants to evolve to the higher state of thinking—to the seventh level—he must grant his Masters and Teachers access to his mind more often through meditation and prayer. The time for this resolution is right now, for tomorrow may never occur. Allow us to invest our years of searching and studying for the *Truths*; allow us to insert our dissertations into your mind. We who have gathered around you today declare this to be a joint effort.

Seek the Hidden Truths

Ishmael, who directs this energy, is an intelligent and brilliant spirit and his light shines brightly into all of us as well as you. He has again been reviewing with us an area concerning the mind that is hidden from sight, so to speak, that region which holds the secrets of *Truths* learned centuries ago. The lack of this wisdom on the earth today is evidence that this wisdom remains hidden until man's mind is somehow activated sufficiently to regenerate (that is, locate and stir up again) these obscured thoughts. No man living on earth today completely understands all of the Father's *Truths*, but once in a while, some of the *Original Truths* do come forward into man's conscious mind.

A Time For Everything

Think Only of Death When the Time Comes

"Mankind seeks a haven within the Father's light." There, and only there, is a haven provided for His children. Remember, my child, He excludes no one individual. The Father tells us continually, "All are My children." We are taught that we are remiss if we single

out one person to dislike. We have for centuries used the excuse of self-defense for the cause of our disliking our foe.

In the universe, oxygen is set free for us to breathe. Our health depends on the amount that we consume. Where does it state, where is it written, how much oxygen a man needs to successfully fulfill his time on the earth? It would stand to reason that we must have learned this from having lived on the earth in some other or some previous lifetime. When and how did we learn to breathe and to accept the correct amount of oxygen?

The Years After Maturity

The master plan for all mankind contains an eventide. If man lives to be old, we here feel we have succeeded in helping him fulfill his destiny—if it is God's will—for it is hoped that by the time man reaches the golden years of old age, he will have fulfilled his covenant he was sent to fulfill. If he does not accomplish that which he came to do, he will simply return to the other side owing rather than our owing him. One should strive to have us owe him, and the best way to accomplish that is to let go of fighting life, and accept it—and learn to accept it on a day-to-day basis.

Do Not Concentrate Upon Death

Mankind should not salute death each moment of his life on earth, rather to think of it only when the Master of Truth says, "Now is the time to come with Me." As man progresses in his lifetime, it is hoped that he would learn how to temper his thoughts and focus more on *Truth Everlasting*. There is a time to play, a time to live, a time to think and a time to repent or feel remorse. All of these occur in specific time periods. Ranking high among those times of life is the time to die.

Man should salute the Lord each morning and

seriously try not to condemn any man. By condemning man, he is also condemning the Lord. You see, each man shares the Lord's light—each and every man. There are no exceptions—not for race, color or creed— <u>all</u> have the Lord's light within them.

Learn to salute the Father each morning. Then enjoy each moment in your lifetime together with the Father. He educates us to enjoy ourselves amid great depressions, amid great wars or happenstance that change our lives. It all depends upon your explicit faith. Yes, if you have enough faith in the Father, you can observe good brought forth from evil.

<u>A Time for Everything</u>

According to the *Truths* that we have been taught for centuries, there is a time for everything. We chose a certain time to be born, and that becomes the most important date in the Julian calendar. Then, there is the time to die, but we have agreed to that time <u>before</u>

birth. Since we agreed to die at a certain time, we then have to obey the Father's orders to come back when He beckons to us. We have to discipline our minds to accept His will. Mankind finds that very difficult to do at times. We must understand this is a *Truth* that has been agreed upon by all mankind with the Father. Each man truly understands when it is his time to return.

Now let us rethink what we have just said: If we choose to live beyond the set time we had agreed to live upon the earth, how do we advise the Father that we have changed our minds?

Remember, my child, there is an interim time set for all of mankind. Had he indeed fulfilled all of his duties and promises on the earth, he could exit ahead of schedule. Because of this, there is a certain interim time when the *Soldiers of Truth* come forth to review our progress. If man has not progressed according to his given schedule of time, he must remain living on the earth until he finishes the work that was originally planned that he must accomplish. If, however, the interim time period comes earlier than he originally planned to return <u>and</u> if he has already finished all he had promised, then he may recant his original time and come back to live even closer to the Father than ever before.

If man wishes to extend his time simply because he wants to spend more time with his family, the Father will advise him that he cannot extend his time and that for all the compassion that the Father might feel in His heart for the man and his family, he still must proceed with the original schedule at the planned time.

Now to reverse this position: If man wanted to die earlier than he had promised to do, all he would have to do is consult with his Master Teachers and advise them that he no longer feels that he can abide living on the earth and that he feels he could not finish his mission, no matter the time allotted. He will ask, "Will you please take me safely back home?" The Teachers of Truth will look over his life record to see if he has amassed enough light to return. They simply measure his effect upon the earth, his efforts to help others and his efforts to fulfill his proposed destiny. His time may be escalated so he will be allowed to return to the Father if he has accumulated enough light.

We must be truthful; that does not often happen for most men wish to remain alive longer than they are destined to live. To avoid this holocaust because of man's fear of dying, he must examine his motives to see why he wants to continue to live longer. Very often when asked about this, man will answer by saying, "I fear leaving the earth." If you feel fear of dying, we— your Masters—will continue working with you to help rid yourself of that fear. This is why you notice most people will appear to be so quiet and peaceful before they draw their last breath. You must return without fear within your hearts and souls. When you learn how to overcome fear, you lose that sense of guilt so many humans carry around. It is only with the loss of fear that you are able to reverse the procedure and you no longer fear death.

Without fear, man can dare negative forces to come near him. Man says, "I shall send you unto the Father's light." That scares and halts the negative force and it will not bother man again; for in man's daring the negativity to reveal itself, the negative force becomes afraid and hastily retreats into darkness. You see, my child, negativity lives off of the fear that grows within man's mind. You can only chastise negativity by saying, "I shall send your thoughts directly to the Father's light." All fear and all negativity leave so man is freed.

You must teach these thoughts and live them on a daily basis. It will help mankind find happiness and joy on the earth.

<u>Fear of Dying Is Unnecessary</u>

The following is one of our prayers: *"Blessed is the man who soothes another's heart."*

Today we wish to speak upon a subject which sometimes triggers fright into the heart of mankind; but as we go along, we will learn that fear is not necessary. It only occurs because of the ignorance of man.

We attempt, as human beings, to resign from the human race when we feel inadequate, unwanted and unloved. These feelings cause us to want to destroy our very own life. Education alone stimulates the mind, reminding each of us of our chosen purpose while living on the earth. The human race differs from the animal kingdom in that animals do not fret about their destiny. It is amazing how men all around the world hope to attract attention to what they consider is their plight— meaning, of course, this fear of death. This seems to monopolize their minds, not allowing them to fulfill the destiny that they came to do. On the other hand, the animal kingdom rarely imposes a sentence of death upon its fellow members. They all cling to life, enjoying whatever is meted out to them. What seems to matter most to them is that they want to simply impart their good upon the earth and then simply return through the veil on their future journey under a new and higher level of consciousness.

In the beginning, when mankind agreed to return to dwell upon the earth to fulfill the mission left undone, he vowed to set his mind free to soar and allow it to feel a release from life's tragedy and suffering. In this way, we all hope to dispel the gloom that accompanies death. Yes, death seems to inspire fear of the unknown. Indeed, it is often the quiet time that is so disquieting to man, that unknown area or quality of life that faces him on the other side of the veil.

Many times we have reminded you that there is as much evil as good within man and that man must acquaint himself with evil so that he can ascertain the difference when good or evil presents itself. When the time comes to leave the earth, he will know better than to follow the negative light.

When man regains his equilibrium on the other side, he assesses the value of *Truth* and strives to live on the upper crescent of the moon. Yes, my child, when you live close to the Lord, He sees and knows your heartaches and He alleviates them for you so that you can follow only His light and not that of a negative spirit.

Our advice to man is <u>fear not</u> as you live your life upon earth. All Masters and Teachers who have helped you during your lifetime will again await you and will instruct you about how to face life in the hereafter.

Man's Gifts

Every man is born with a gift. It is a gift of service. We were all sent to perform certain gifts of service. Some may be physical, others spiritual. The gift does not matter. Whether it is a clerk, an engineer, a handyman or a spiritual teacher, all are of equal value in the sight of God in the universe. Each of us brings a gift. The way we use our gift and its quality are the important part of life.

Each man possessing the spiritual gift may be asked to help a loved one to die or to help him go from this state of being into another. At that time we must let go of the pain, anguish and suffering of losing a loved one. This is a difficult task but a very necessary one in order to bring peace and harmony to the one who is about to depart. You must replace their anguish with a peace and a quiet from within yourself and then, with all of the love and compassion you can muster, you must say, "It is the time to go, my loved one. Just let go knowing you are loved by all of us and all who wait to greet you on your return home. Now, go toward the light, go quietly, go lightly—go toward the light."

The *Eternal Truth* is that there is no final death and that love is the unifying force of this cosmic world. This knowledge and attitude helps to overcome men's fears and helps them to reach out in helpfulness to others in such times as when we have periods of floods, earthquakes and wars.

When sincere seekers search for the purpose of their earthly existence, all men reach identical conclusions—regardless of their religious training, personal philosophies, color or creeds—and that is that life continues to exist beyond so-called death. They learn that love, mutual respect and helpfulness are the keys to spiritual growth.

Man must always remember that prayer is a

powerful force for good and that life is eternal.

As We Live on Earth

So We Live in the Hereafter

Before we start our conversation with you today, we think man could better understand his life on earth if he understood that living on earth is like going to school every day. For each day, he learns how to solve each problem as it presents itself. This leads us into our discussion on how his present life affects his life in the hereafter.

The first word we want to bring to you is the word "perseverance." Men who live on the earth today do not understand the true meaning of this word. If man learns to persevere, soon all common matters will be healed or worked out. Perseverance is deemed necessary for this earthly existence. Allowing that this is true, we must begin to take the thoughts that are placed into our minds and think them through to fruition. What makes existence on the earth necessary is that you have to learn how to exist down on the earth in order to learn how to live in the <u>hereafter</u>. Following this assumption, who among us is not willing to endure a little despair or a little hardship in order to live happily in the hereafter?

Let us explore further this theory about *Life Everlasting*. Who among us knows the purpose that has been designed for us to fulfill while we live on the earth? Who among us allows our thought process to persevere enough in our daily lives to truly learn our real purpose? These types of questions should be found in every man's thoughts, but when we investigated, we found that the man of today wants instant gratification. He is not concerned about learning from each experience or determining the reason for the experience nor the lesson to be learned therefrom. Man wants to live his life tastefully, with all the necessities and niceties, but when he suddenly finds himself upon his return to the other side of the curtain in the hereafter, he complains bitterly to himself. He says to himself, "Why could I not have made the Lord the center of my attention from my earliest recollection so that I could salute Him each morning and have made Him and His *laws* a part of my daily life? If I had only obeyed the *laws*, my immortality could have been a blessed event. But there always seemed to be more pressing issues that needed my care and time."

While we live on earth, we should wish <u>each person</u> that we meet along the way a good day. We should not concentrate on wishing him a long life but rather concentrate on the quality of life, for the time is allotted to him one day at a time.

We must learn to express our willingness to accede to the covenant we had promised to fulfill and we should begin by asking, "What is Your wish for me today, Father? I want only Thy will to be done." A person should then feel a sense of relief when he hears the voice within echoing:

"My child, what is necessary for you to do today is to extend yourself beyond your own expectations and be not afraid to ask for help when it is needed. Remember always to reach out to help others as well by extending your hand to them—especially at times of need. You will be doubly blessed by teaching them how to help themselves."

We have an affirmation that will help you carry on during times of travail: *"I feel closer to the Lord today than ever before. I know He is with me always."*

The sage advice for man is to take time and re-evaluate himself often by asking, *"Have I fulfilled my covenant, Father? If I have not, please guide me back to my pathway so that I can find my way."* The covenant was made in the very beginning of time and will continue until the end of time. It is a promise you made to our beloved Father.

PASSING INTO THE HEREAFTER

Need For Light And Energy

My child, I have often wanted to talk to you about this topic. I should like to pass on this information to your class and to all who will listen, for it is very important information that all men should know.

When we live life to its completion, we come to a very wide river. That is when we first leave the earth. The first plane of thinking provides us with enough light to follow the trail that leads us to make other decisions. As an example, "Do we live here or in the Land of Lore?" Thus man waits a while longer and thinks upon this question; and because we have expended the energy to regenerate more energy by thinking, we are then taken to the Land of Lore. But first, we have to cross the river. We have very often spoken to you about how deep is down. Now that pertains to the river of life. Occasionally we master enough energy or light to force ourselves over it, across it, or pass it by. The answer is determined by how long we have lived with and through the Lord's light.

Crossing the Sea of Life

The depth of the sea (one's mind or consciousness) can be filled with such debris caused by idle thoughts, refusal to learn the truth and other troubles that we have carried forward with us. As you can see, if the sea is full of debris, it will make it very difficult to swim across. Many men live entire lifetimes without accepting any responsibility for fulfilling their destiny. They continuously clog their minds with material and carnal fulfillment, never attempting to learn or gain any spiritual knowledge; therefore, they never earn any additional light or energy. By keeping their minds so clogged with their everyday nonsensical and irresponsible thinking, they fill the sea of life with debris of such huge amounts that they are unable to cross the sea of life. As a result, they must relive and relive their lives until finally they reach the sea and find it clear and thus they are able to go on. If, on the other hand, we see the sea is clear and clean, then we have learned; we have gained the necessary energy to cross. It means our minds have been freed and cleared; thus we are able to glide across and flow with the tide. In the event that occurs, it takes us even closer to the Father.

Another interpretation is simple: We find the sea of life. Once we cross over and if we have earned sufficient light energy to manipulate ourselves across, we are led directly to the Father's light. If this does not occur, we have to maintain a peaceful decorum about ourselves until we can accumulate enough light or energy to make it across the sea of life.

The standards are different for each person because each person's purpose is different—some needing more light or energy than others even at the onset because men have evolved to different vibration levels. Man has to stand close to the Lord when he returns and he rewards the Lord by bringing back the original amount of light or energy plus that which he has gained during his present lifetime. Man must amass enough light to climb to the top of the mountain for, remember, he must scale it only after crossing the sea of life. Many lifetimes can go by until his wisdom reacts to this knowledge fed to him through the Lord's light and lessons. It can take many lifetimes before one man can compile the necessary light and energy he can need to heed the Lord's lessons correctly. Mankind has to live continually until they learn how to maneuver themselves to the top of the mountain after crossing the stream of life.

Let man live in peace; as long as he has generated enough light, he will be able to scramble to the top of the mountain. There at long last he has amassed the energy that the Lord originally sent him back home to amass. That would mean enough energy to cross the ocean blue of life and amass enough energy to climb the highest mountain of the enlightened heights of wisdom which only the Lord understands.

Only the Lord understands the depth of the mind of the lion as well as the depth of the sea of life. Only when we have generated the necessary energy does the Lord accept us back with willing and aching heart because He loves us all and waits patiently for us to cross life's ocean and to climb the highest mountain top.

Experiencing Death

It is important to remember that education eliminates the negative forces involving our lifetime of fear of the unknown. How man accepts his own death or fear of death is experienced differently by each of us. Fear of death causes man to use his mind in an unwise manner and only education eliminates the thoughts of fear, of misconceived things that could happen. The unwise use of man's mind is the reason we wish to bring the illumination of thoughts today to help man overcome this great fear. We are trying to extinguish the fear that we find within man's mind. We are trying to remind man that fear compounds itself, that no man, no *Master of Truth*, can eliminate all the fears that man allows to compound within his own mind. He has to learn how to eliminate this negative force that possesses him.

We would advise man to sit down and concentrate and not allow his mind to run wild with fear in anticipation of death. Man should instead acquaint himself with the hereafter. You say, "How can this be?"

Well, this is the way: A man should sit down and visualize his own position of power in the hereafter. He will soon be able to reason that death as an end to all things is merely a myth; that actually, it is a fleeting, passing, passive sensation that eliminates all the negative forces that strive to propel man into a mighty juggernaut which does not release him beyond the border of his own mind.

In passing, he suddenly sees the image of the Father within his own mind. He hears the Father saying to him, *"Calm your mind down and accept the fact that I am here."* Sooner or later a fearful man will betray his own feelings and see the Father there before his very eyes. Through that manifestation of *Truth*, he begins to realize and accept the fact that he is no longer among the living earthlings and that there is nothing to fear for the Father is with him.

When Man Passes Over, He Meets Familiars

By visualizing all of this and coming to terms with this fact, man gains acceptance and can eliminate the excess fear that he carried about death and then he relaxes and begins to notice things floating around him. He wonders, "Who is this? What is this exactly? Where am I?" Did he not do the same thing when he lived on the earth? Did man not ask himself, "Why am I here? Who am I? What is my purpose on earth?" Then he queried of himself, "In what direction should I look? What direction should I take?" Suddenly, beyond his wildest expectations, he sees familiar faces, some from olden days, some from this, his most recent lifetime. He recognizes men and women, but he hesitates to say anything to them for fear they will abruptly disappear. But then, just as suddenly, they begin communicating with him on a mental level, and they are saying, "Welcome, child. Come farther into the escalation of time. Yes, we are beyond your time, so adjust your mind and sort out fact from fancy and come forth to greet us."

He begins to relax his mind, and he asks of these familiar faces, "How do I do that? How can I reach up to you?" As quietly as a whisper, they say, "You must stick to facts and not falter and release all cares." And then again, he asks, "How do I do that?" Again they answer, "Come farther into this escalating world, for it is insulated from troubles and cares. You must leave all of those thoughts behind. The loved ones you leave behind can care for themselves. Their troubles will multiply so that they might learn their lessons until they cease to live on the earth. Now, compare your thinking with that of those who still live on the earth. Is it similar? If it is, you must still stay close to the earth. When you release the avenging fears and other troubling thoughts, then your mind will be free so that you can accompany us and adjust your thinking. Do that soon for we wait patiently to talk and visit with you."

Preparation on the Earth for Passing

Now, this is exactly the way it happens on the earth while man still lives. He must acquaint himself with his Masters and Teachers through meditation, and know and love his loved ones. For when he ceases to live, he does not extend his hand to his loved ones on the earth. He instead accepts the hands of his beloved who preceded him in death. When he adjusts his thinking as we have described thus far to you, his mind aches no more and his body trembles no more. He has fulfilled his earthly duties, and thus he forgives all of mankind— no longer accusing anyone of injustice toward him. He simply has slipped into oblivion with his own kind.

This is a simple message of *Truth* brought to you to help you assuage your fears and the fears of mankind about death. We have tried to describe to you how and what to expect once you reach the other side. This also serves as an exercise in solution only, an admonition to those who seek the higher sources of life but who continue to live with fear in their hearts. Allow people to know that death is a simple function, that they experience no pain, and that no evil follows them unless their minds are harnessed with evil thoughts.

CHAPTER 15

PRAYERS FOR EACH DAY

<u>Morning Prayers</u>

Thank You, Dear Father, for seeing me through the night. Thank You for talking to me and teaching me throughout the night. May Your infinite wisdom touch and spark my soul into understanding and acceptance of that which I am destined to be.

Amen

Dear God, bless my efforts this day. Let me make the most of all opportunities You choose to send me. Give me, Father, all the things I need for this day.

Amen

"The God in me can accomplish and overcome whatever I may face this day, for I am a part of all that is.   Amen"

"O Holy Father reckon unto me today Guide and reckon with me in Thy manner or Thy way.   Amen"

"May God bless the efforts of this day I surrender myself in Your keeping bless my decisions lead me to my highest good bend me, make me into the pattern You have made for me.   Amen"

"Infinite spirit, open the way for great abundance for me for I am an irresistible magnet for good. I ask only for that which belongs to me by divine right.
                                        Amen"

"God let my lips speak Your words,....Let my mind think Your thoughts,....Let my heart feel Your love then my Lord can I say for this day I give thanks...I have lived it Your way.   *Amen"*

"Take me safely home to Thee, Father, and exchange energy with me so that I may exist in peace with good health and happiness and an abundance of what I need, that I may fulfill my lifetime here on the earth plane.   *Amen"*

Evening Prayers

"Dear Father, the giver of all light, please help me. Many times I have strayed from the path, but I continue to love You, and I earnestly beseech You to guide and help me. I promise to try to listen to hear that which You have to say, and to live Your laws. I am learning to forgive myself and to love myself, for through this demonstration of caring, I know You have forgiven me.

Amen"

"Thank You, Father, for the blessings of this day. Protect me and keep me through the night. Amen"

"Holy Father, help us all find the pathway that leads easily back home to Thee and protect my soul through the night.

And now that I am entering Heaven may I also cheer myself up by saying there will be enough light for all of us...in Heaven as well as on earth.

Amen"

Prayers For Everyday Living

"O Father, Master of the universe give us the peace of mind to understand and to live our lives through to the very end without hatred or negativity of any kind.

Lead and direct us along life's highway without one thought of envy or hatred.

Garner for us the skylight that we need to maintain evenness within our own lives and teach us equally how to sustain ourselves and those that we love.

Covet us close to Thy heart and even though I stumble

and fall...help me up and help me to educate myself along that highway of life so that material things will not count for my whole life...just enough to assemble a living for myself and my family.

Let me tithe my income so that when the end comes I can say 'Father, I tithed so that my brothers and sisters could also have something that was needed on earth,'

Amen

"Take me back safely, Father. Teach me the rudiments of truth. Allow me to follow the pathway we have set for ourselves with Your blessings, Father!

Amen"

"God, send me the power of believing and the proof of my convictions.   *Amen"*

"Almighty Lord, Father of the universe, we seek the wonderment and radiance of Your light for us all, so that we may dispense it among mankind.

Amen"

"Father, teach me the truthful path to life Everlasting. Award me happiness. Please hear me.

Amen"

"Please, Father, I do not pray for tomorrow, but this is what I need today. Please provide for me today.

Amen"

The love of God always surrounds me, the power of God will protect me, the presence of God watches over me, the wisdom of God guides me; wherever I am, God is also.

Amen

"Teach me O Father to love that I might create beauty, health, happiness and material worth for all of Your children as well as myself.   Amen"

"May God bless each man who teaches His words, who listens to them and who tries to fully understand them, for as the Lord walks beside thee each morning of your life, bless Him and thus bring blessings into your life.   Amen"

"Help us, O Heavenly Father, help us understand Your lessons. Help us to understand the depth of Your thinking from the very beginning of time until the very end. Help us, O Father; have mercy in Your heart and help us find our way back to Thee.

          Amen"

"Almighty Father, Blessed Angel of Truth, include me in Your daily thoughts. Excuse me; forgive me if I do not praise You enough. I stare off into space not knowing the Truth that You are there also. I speculate upon the mysteries of the universe; yet, I do not have to speculate because You relate them and explain all of the so-called mysteries to me. Why then do I not relate these things--these mysteries--of Your thinking? Should I not recognize Your thoughts as equal unto mine? Should I not understand that my thoughts are indeed Your thoughts from the very beginning?   *Amen"*

"Almighty Father of the Universe, help us select the right thoughts for our minds to absorb. Let us envision Truths only so that we might conduct our lives in the rightful manner.   *Amen."*

"Please give me back my direction to the Laws of the Universe. Set me free again to understand Thy ways and thoughts. Amen."*

"Show me the way, Father. I must learn to trust in Your instructions and in Your instincts completely. Thus, I shall never know fear as I know You are ever present to help me avoid the pitfalls and holocausts that come into man's life. Amen"*

"I feel blessed by Thee, Lord. I feel blessed by Thee. I am willing to abdicate control over my entire life. Thus, all of my problems that I have wrestled unsuccessfully with, I offer and give to You. Therefore, I truly feel blessed, O Lord. I feel blessed, sad as I have felt; now I feel glee for I know that You will work

everything out and make it all right again. When I bless Thee, O Lord, I also feel truly blessed.   *Amen."*

"Allow us the freedom, O Lord, to live in Your sunlight which You and You alone possess. Give to us the understanding to separate Truth from evil, to sort out the fiction from the fact and allow us Your love by giving us the privilege of knowing Your love even more intimately and intently. O Father, give to us the illumination we need to understand Thy words. Father of Mercy, allow us happiness and joy. Allow us the education we need to survive during this lifetime. Help us by renewing our energy daily and giving to us the strength of character that we need to succeed in this lifetime.   *Amen."*

"I am here Father gathered together with your children, lead us out of the wilderness and darkness to our destiny, to the light. Lead us out of trouble to the greener pastures promised to us. Guide and direct our lives, Oh Father, for You are the one and only God over all mankind. Amen"

"Teach me the truthful path to life everlasting. Award me happiness. Please hear me. Amen"

"Beloved Father, come into my life, seek me out and help me to find the happiness and joy that You promised me from the very beginning of time. And please, O Heavenly Father, take away all negative thoughts, replacing them with Truth, happiness and joy. Amen."

"Help us, O Lord, to find the happiness and joy we need to feel in this lifetime; help us to learn how to comfort the poor, the lame of the body, of the heart, of the spirit and of the soul.   *Amen"*

A HEALING PRAYER

"I feel badly about what has happened to me, but I accept it and want to go on living within my haven of refuge until finally all cells interact, not in a negative way, but only in a good and positive health-giving manner. Please, O Heavenly Father, direct my energy within my cells to respond to this way of thinking so that I might accept life and know in truth the meaning of '<u>heal thyself</u>.'   *Amen"*

AFFIRMATIONS

"There is but One Presence, One Power, One Substance, One Law in the universe and I am one with all there is.

"I am one with the Father with whom I live, He lives in my mortal temple, therefore, I shall lack for nothing, ever.

"I am God's child; nothing can harm me!

"I can do this. I want to do this; therefore with the Father's light, I <u>can</u> do this."

"He will help me. He will guide and direct me."

"As a man thinketh, so he is."

"I am God's child; no harm can come to me."

"This is going to be the best day of my life!"

"Here I am, Father, take me back home to Thee anew."

"I will live close to the Father daily. I will sense His will. I will sense His thinking. Trouble cannot come into my life as long as the Father assures me of this truth, for then I can assure myself of a happy life without fear. My life shall be an example among mankind. No harm can come into my life. He lives close to me, to show me the way out of all my troubles. I evince no fear, for the Lord watches over me."

AID FOR SLEEPING

"I see tremendous colored balloons filled with helium. These balloons are carrying all of my troubles, all of my frustrations, all of my heartache up and away. These balloons float higher and higher away from me until the sky is a clear blue. Now, I am free and have no fears."

THE WORDS THE FATHER TAUGHT US WHEN FIRST HE PLACED US UPON THE EARTH

"If you will live together as I have placed you and care for one another, love one another, and take on the troubles of one another, then truly you shall learn and you shall live the Laws, and you shall return safely back home to Me."

"You shall remain alive upon the Earth and roam the face of the Earth until you have mastered every word

of My original Teachings.

"In My parting words I say to you again: You are to live together; you are to be responsible one for the other; you are to treat each other as you would have yourself treated; and you shall love your fellowman with all your heart you shall remain alive on the Earth until you have learned and lived My Laws."

"Abide within Me, live with Me. Rejoice, for I am within your aching heart, within the widow's weeds and I shall continue to sit alongside thee until the end of time everlasting. Just come unto Me."

"Do unto others as you would have them do unto thee."

GUIDING THOUGHTS FOR DAILY LIVING

Start each day with a positive attitude toward life...Start each day with this thought: "This day is a new beginning for the rest of my life...Now I am going to reassess and re-evaluate my feelings, my thoughts as well as my goals.

Yesterday is gone, I cannot change that but I can try to make this day a better one and learn from every day.

Reach out to help someone each day. Make a conscious effort to do so...God will bless you many many times for caring for His children.

Each morning assess your desire for life. Wake up with great zest for living. Make it all worthwhile for always remember that many would give all they own to change places with you, just to be able to get up and go.

Live a divine life... Seek it, Desire it and try to live as divine a life as possible.

Use a higher plane of thinking but make it a happy one. Happiness and joy belongs to each man, it was a promise made to us in the very beginning.

Always allow your mind to wander and dream. Practice doing this carefully and as often as possible then this will help you to direct and realize your destiny.

Allow your mind to wander even out of your brain and your body so to speak...Let it flit about from subject to subject. It helps you to realize what you want to do and until you realize that you cannot fulfill your *destiny...It also helps you to realize your desires and if they fit into your pattern of life, God will make them come about.*

Learn how to project your mind further...Allow your Masters time each day to understand your thinking...Communicate with them...allow them time to assess your desires...Allow them time to acquaint themselves with you as well as your temperament so that they can soothe your weary heart and soul. That helps them to guide and direct your energy for the events coming into this lifetime.

Educate your mind to hold a thought, one simple thought...Bring it to fruition and fulfillment by allowing your Masters and Teachers to investigate your dreams and hopes, they then can instill into your mind peace and heaven on earth.

Acceptance of life, of course, is the secret of life. Accepting that which you cannot change and making the effort to change that which you can.

The most important thing is to put yourself into Gods hands.

"I celebrate life, Father. I thank You for my health, my happiness and my joy. I celebrate life because You have helped me expand my consciousness so that I have no fear of living while on the Earth. Help me by guiding me so that I do not stumble and fall. Show me the way that I might share any rewards or any of Your manifestations of Truth with all of mankind."

"I will not allow anything to bother me. I will accede to God's wishes and be content. I will live in

Peace and harmony with those around me, however, it might be more simple to live in disharmony."

When you think a negative thought say: "This does not belong to me; this is alien to me. Cancel it. Cancel it."

"I forgive those who would harm me, and I will not allow myself to think upon them."

"I hate no man. I permit everyone his freedom, but I ignore deceitful people."

"I exist in spirit now; I am allowing my spirit--my soul--to soar. Now I shall listen to the still, small voice within---that of my higher self I shall feel and sense great love. I shall not allow myself to harbor any resentment against any person or for any cause to disturb me whatsoever."

"Oh God, give me the grace and the foresight to learn by this experience."

"No, I reject your negative vibrations. I pray for your salvation but I do not allow you to distress me further." Say, "Please, God, forgive that man for trying to make my life miserable. Allow me to forgive and forget."

"I don't want ill health or any harm to come to this person. I want only this person's happiness.

"Father, teach me to dispel this hurt from my mind."

"Here on earth I am happy, I salute the Lord Himself for His mercy shines down upon this earth plane for us all."

"I observe these laws of truth. I am rewarded by

the Masters of Truth. Now I shall observe these thoughts whenever I am displeased by any negative thought. I shall wipe it out of my mind by observing the universe and its laws."

"I shall allow myself to see the stars bright at night. I shall observe and respect the heavens above me studded with stars that illuminate the way safely back home to the Father."

"I shall observe His laws. My destiny depends upon my observing these laws. I will sense a new beginning for the universe as well as for myself as I observe the laws, as I progress on my way down the pathway of life."

"Teach me the rudiments of truth. Allow me to follow the pathway we have set for ourselves with your blessings, Father!"

"Regardless of how difficult my life becomes, I only want Your ideas, Your guidance, and Your advice. I shall try to live this life You have given to me to the best of my knowledge and ability."

"Come back into my life, O merciful Father, and take this evil thought out of my mind. Do not allow it to attach itself unto me for I fear if evil involved me further into its grasp, I might remain alive forever on this Earth without fulfilling my mission. Please take away the hurt and the heartache that I might feel peace. And please, Father, rejoice with me that I understand how to dispose of this evil and the woe-begotten thoughts. Unlike other men, I rejoice in You, Father, and I gather my energy each morning through Your light. This I know and I rejoice within my heart and soul knowing full well that You are the Almighty Father over all of mankind and *that You would not release unfit or misspent energy into my mind.*   *Amen."*

"I give praise and thanks to Thee, Oh Father, that You are bringing forth this perfect picture to me. I know it pleases You to see Your children happy, healthy, with peace of mind. Teach me, Oh Father, to love, that I might create beauty, health, happiness and material worth for all of Your children, as well as myself"

THE LORDS PRAYER

OUR FATHER, WHO ART IN HEAVEN HALLOWED BE THY NAME.

THY KINGDOM COME- THY WILL BE DONE ON EARTH AS IT IS IN HEAVEN.

GIVE US THIS DAY OUR DAILY BREAD AND GIVE US THE SPIRIT AND THE LIGHT TO FORGIVE OUR OWN INADEQUACIES AS WE PROPOSE TO FORGIVE ALL OTHERS.

LEAD US OUT OF THE DARKNESS AND WILDERNESS, INTO THE LIGHT....

FOR THINE IS THE KINGDOM,

 THE POWER,

 AND THE GLORY...

 FOREVER AND EVER.

AMEN

MORE SPIRITUAL TRUTHS AVAILABLE
FROM PESHA PUBLISHING

#1.. Additional copies of ***How To Find Your Way Back Home.*** Price..$16.95 + $3 for shipping and handling **Total = $19.95.**

#2.. Copies of Bess's other book...***Heaven On Earth Is A Mission.*** Price $16.95 + $3 for shipping and handling **Total = $19.95.**

#3.. *THE MASTERS SERIES* (Part **#1)** **Choose audiocassettes or CD's. This program was recorded in Bess's own voice.**

Tape #1- FEAR, Bess will discuss with you how to deal with and **overcome your greatest fears in life.**

Tape #2- PURPOSE, Bess speaks about this **most important aspect** of anyone's life.

Tape #3- HAPPINESS, **A quality of life that every person wants.** Do you know how to achieve it?

Tape #4- HOW TO FACE LIFE EACH DAY, Bess will give you some ideas about how to start and keep your day running with **less stress.**

Tape #5- SEVEN STEPS TO PERFECTION, Since all people have frailties, this tape will help motivate you to strive a little harder and **forgive yourself** a little more.

Tape #6- HEALING, In a most **fascinating** fashion Bess will walk you through a session of how to **help your body heal itself.** These techniques have been used for centuries. These methods are not meant to be used to replace modern medicine, only to compliment it.

You may purchase the tapes or CD's for $39.95 and for a limited time we pay all your shipping and handling charges.

TO ORDER:

SEND a check or money order to:

PESHA PUBLISHING-
P.O. BOX 47484

PHOENIX, AZ 85068-7484

PLEASE INCLUDE:

Your complete (PRINTED) shipping address

A description of the product you are ordering and if you want tapes or CD's and a telephone number or e-mail address in case of a problem with shipping.

OR you can ORDER AT OUR WEBSITE

www.peshaonline.com

You can check the website for any new material.

ALL INFORMATION IS CONFIDENTIAL

AND WILL ONLY BE USED BY

PESHA PUBLISHING.